Longing for the Sea and Yet Not Afraid

This booklet contains transcripts, not reviewed by the speakers, of talks given at New York Encounter 2016

Crossroads Cultural Center

Transcriptions by Karen Kaffenberger
Copyediting and layout by Deep River Media, LLC

Human Adventure Books

Longing for the Sea and Yet (Not) Afraid
Proceedings of New York Encounter 2016
Crossroads Cultural Center

Longing for the Sea and yet Afraid

We embark on the journey of life spurred by a promise of happiness in our heart. But then, fear of the unknown makes us hesitant, especially if the destination is not certain. Desire choked by fear appears to be the common experience of our time.

We strive to build relationships and overcome divisions, and yet we end up stifling true dialogue, due to preconceptions or conformity to the demands of political correctness. We dream of achieving greatness in some dimension of our lives, and yet we settle for a comfortable life. We ache for something new (and constantly check our smart phones in expectation), and yet we abhor events that are out of our control. We crave stability, but we are unsure that what is true today will still be true tomorrow. We strive to be more "mindful" in the present, and yet our mind is always fleeing from the here and now. We desire belonging, and yet we dread relinquishing our freedom. We long to encounter a lover, a friend, a father who will break through our radical solitude, and yet we are afraid of losing ourselves.

We long to sail on the sea of life and yet we are afraid of leaving our safe harbor.

What is the final word on man's desire? Is there an attraction capable of overcoming our fears and drawing us out to the open waters that our hearts yearn for?

"The 'I' finds itself again when it encounters a presence
that brings this announcement:
'What your heart is made for does exist!'"
(L. Giussani)

CONTENTS

NEW YORK
ENCOUNTER

Spurred by the Promise of Happiness

The Encounter opens with poetry, music, and a conversation with ***Christian Wiman****, poet and Senior Lecturer, Yale Divinity School, and* ***Greg Wolfe****, Editor of* Image

Introduction

"When the Italian writer Cesare Pavese won the most highly-prized Italian literary award, the Premio Strega, he commented:

'You also have the gift of fertility. You are the master of yourself, of your fate. You are as famous as any man can be who does not seek to be so. Yet, all that will come to an end. This profound joy of yours, this glow of super-abundance, is made of things you did not take into account. It was given to you. By whom? "Whom should you thank? Whom will you curse when it all disappears?"

And, on the day he received the Premio Strega, he wrote: 'I have just come back from Rome. In Rome, apotheosis. But now, this is it.' However, already in the first entries of his diary, we find an observation of prime value: 'What a great thought it is that truly nothing is due to us. Has anyone ever promised us anything? Then, why should we expect anything?'Perhaps he did not realize that Expectation is the very structure of our nature, it is the essence of our soul. It is not something calculated: it is given. For the promise is at the origin, from the very origin of our creation. He who has made man has also made him as 'promise.' Structurally man waits; structurally he is a beggar; structurally life is a promise."
(Msgr. Luigi Giussani, *The Religious Sense*, McGill-Queen's University Press, 1997)

Friday, January 15, 2016

Wolfe: I'm very glad to be here. My name is Gregory Wolfe, and I'm the editor of *Image*, a journal of arts and literature as they encounter the religious traditions of Western civilization—Judaism, Christianity, and Islam. I'm very pleased to be here tonight to be factotum and interviewer-in-chief for Christian Wiman.

Christian Wiman is the author, editor, and translator of nine books. His most recent is a prose book, *My Bright Abyss: Meditations of a Modern Believer*, which the *New Republic* called "an apologia and a prayer, an invitation and a fellow-traveler for any who suffer and all who believe." His most recent book of poems is *Once in the West*; his previous collection, *Every Riven Thing*, won the Ambassador Award and was named one of the best books of the year by *The New Yorker*.

Of his work as a whole, Marilynne Robinson writes: "His poetry and scholarship have a purifying urgency that is rare in this world. This puts him at the very source of theology, and enables him to say things in timeless language, so that the reader's surprise and assent are one and the same."

From 2003 until 2013, he was the editor of *Poetry*, the premiere magazine for poetry in the English-speaking world. During his tenure, the magazine's circulation tripled. It garnered two National Magazine Awards from the American Society of Magazine Editors. Mr. Wiman has written for *The New Yorker*, *The New York Times Book Review*, *The Atlantic*, and numerous other publications. He is a former Guggenheim Fellow and holds an honorary Doctorate of Humane Letters from North Central College.

According to his website, his particular interests at the Yale Divinity School, where he teaches, include modern poetry, the language of faith, accidental theology—that is, theology conducted by unexpected means; my favorite kind—and what it means to be a Christian intellectual in a secular culture.

Welcome, Chris.

Wiman: Thank you. [*applause*]

Wolfe: We started off with a poem called "George Gray." It was read so beautifully for us just now and it ended with the line that gives us our theme for the New York Encounter this year. Does it spark any thoughts in you?

Wiman: It does. As I think about it in my own life, I'm struck by how often I can articulate a psychological dilemma, but that being able to articulate it will not rescue me from it. I think that we live in a therapeutic culture. We think if we can just put words on it then we will be released from our tensions; but I often find that's not true. I think what releases me are remembrances of moments when I was released. The great Jewish theologian, Abraham Joshua Heschel, says faith is mostly faithfulness to the times when we had faith, which I think is a wonderful definition, a very hopeful definition. If you find yourself going through life wondering about your faith, then you think, *Well, at one time I must have had it*, and you remain faithful to those moments in your life when you had faith. Edgar Lee Masters is an American poet who makes me think of another poet, A. R. Ammons. I don't have the poem in front of me, but I think I can do it. If I mess up, bear with me. It is sort of perfect for the theme of this conference. The poem is called "The City Limits." The late great poet A.R. Ammons died about thirteen years ago.

When you consider the radiance, that it does not withhold
itself but pours its abundance without selection into every
nook or cranny not overhung or hidden; when you consider

that birds' bones make no awful noise against the light but
lie low in the light as in a high testimony; when you consider
the radiance, that it will look into the guiltiest

swervings of the weaving heart and bear itself upon them,
not flinching into disguise or darkening; when you consider
the abundance of such resource as illuminates the glow-blue

bodies and gold-skeined wings of flies swarming the dumped

guts of a natural slaughter or the coil of shit and in no
way winches from its storms of generosity; when you consider

that air or shale, snow or vacuum, squid or wolf, rose or lichen,
each is accepted into as much light as it will take, then
the heart moves roomier, the man stands and looks about, the

leaf does not increase itself above the grass, and the dark
work of the deepest cells is of a tune with May bushes
and fear lit by the breadth of such calmly turns to praise.

The Masters poem reminds me of the Ammons poem. The Ammons poem is a moment of faith, I think, written by a person who, incidentally, professed not to have any faith.

Wolfe: So, "Longing for the Sea and Yet Not Afraid." There's this word: *longing*. It's a word that you had used yourself, I think, particularly in *My Bright Abyss*. You actually start the book with a short, fragmentary poem, or a poem you call a failed poem, that includes that word *longing*. Some people might use the word *desire* interchangeably with *longing*. What is this longing? What is it in the human heart that seems driven by his desire?

Wiman: I wrote that whole book out of the inability to write a single poem. The fragment of the poem goes: "My God my bright abyss / Into which all my longing will not go / Once more I come to the edge of all I know / And believing nothing believe in this." What? This. I couldn't finish it. A tough poem to finish. What do you believe in? Well, the poem wouldn't finish in years past, and finally I began writing little prose fragments out of the inability, out of this longing to say something, but suffering an inability to know what it was I needed to say. I think the longing is for God. I think we long for a completion that we sense we lack. You mentioned Marilynne Robinson: I am deeply flattered and gratified by the comment she made, because I love her work. In my favorite book of hers, *Housekeeping*, she has this wonderful passage: "Start to imagine a Carthage sown with salt and all the sowers gone, and the seeds lain however long in the earth, till there arose in vegetable profusion a garden of leaves and trees of rime and brine." What flowering could there be in such a garden? And then she goes on to talk about how need can blossom into all the compensations it requires; for when do we know anything so utterly as when we lack it? And here again is a foreshadowing: the world will be made whole. I think a longing, that longing, is a sense of the absolute absence in our lives that has an absolute answer.

Wolfe: Now, a number of people who have encountered your story, even in brief capsule form, know that you have a cancer diagnosis. Many of them who have heard that fact have tended to assume that you turned to religion as a response to that diagnosis. But if I read you correctly in *My Bright Abyss*, it happened a very different way. As I recall, what you say there, you had an experience of falling in love with your wife, the woman who became your wife, Danielle, and you found yourself sitting together moved to pray. So, before we talk about what the illness that you struggled with means to you, why don't we go back to that fundamental experience. Why should love lead to prayer? Why should the experience of falling in love have moved both of you—spontaneously, apparently—to desire this?

Wiman: Yeah, I think we were looking for somebody to thank. You know, when you talk about those moments in your life when you have faith, there are moments when your life seems over the brim, reality seems *more* than reality, and yet still itself by being more than reality, and everyone I know in such moments wants to express gratitude of some sort. There's a wonderful poet I know, Anna Kamieńska, this Polish poet. In her journal she talked about a friend she had, Pietoken, and Pietoken would scrawl "Thank you, God" in the margins of his poems every time he completed one, and he was an avowed atheist. And yet, he still had to thank God for his poems. I think when that happened to me and my wife, we felt so overwhelmed that we wanted someone to thank. It felt like grace. We had no language, or rather, we had lost the language with which to address God; and praying together became a way of trying to do that. Simone Weil has a wonderful line that says, "He who has not felt the presence of God cannot feel his absence," which I have always found to be true.

Wolfe: So it was still a bit of a shock to you, or at least a surprise, for you had at that point not been a religious believer for some time. You were used to moving in a certain literary cultural milieu in which it was pretty odd to find someone with your credentials and your background doing anything as gauche as praying, so how did that happen? I mean, how did you find yourself so surprised by this?

Wiman: You mean what did it look like, or the exact form it took?

Wolfe: Well, I'm just curious. Was it sort of...I mean, I know that you were raised in the faith, so in some sense it was latent in you; you had the memory of this experience growing up in West Texas. Nonetheless, as I gather, it seems to have come as a surprise. If I was you, I would have said, "Oh my God, what is this happening to me?" Like, do I want this to happen?

Wolfe: I kept it at arm's length, any notion of Jesus—until I got sick. I mean getting sick made me need concretely: I needed faith to take concrete form. I needed a church, I needed people, I needed to know why I needed those things. And I hope that if that hadn't happened, I would have made my way to an articulation of faith, but it probably would have been very different.

I don't see any break in my life, in the way that it's been written. I've had people write about me as if there's this huge rift or dividing line, pre- and post-; but if I'm publishing a selection of poems this year and I go in to compile it, then the array of poems would appear to me quite seamless. The things that I was writing about in my first book I was writing about in my third book—the same concerns. The language had changed somewhat, but it was still about longing, it was an inchoate longing that was constantly trying to assume a form.

Wiman: So, if I hear you correctly, it sounds like there was at least a little bit of a shift when you received the cancer diagnosis. Or are you saying that it was more of a theism—a kind of a general belief in God that caused you to want to move towards something more concrete, more palpable—than a movement of some kind?

Wiman: That's absolutely true. Yeah, that's absolutely true. I mean, it was Christ. I could talk to you forever about God, and God is the most ubiquitous word in contemporary poetry. You think that poets are all atheists, but the word *God* is everywhere. Let me tell you, when we got together, when we got ready to do a religious issue of *Poetry* magazine, all we had to do was just do it. I mean, the poems were just flooding in, there were so many poems about God. But what the word means usually is just a sort of sign that says, you know, "This way to the ineffable." It just means nothing. And when I felt my life ending, I needed everything to be concrete. It's a real paradox you know. I'll read you this one poem, which begins: "Love's last urgency is earth." I wrote this poem. I had a bone marrow transplant and I wrote this just before I got the final dose of chemo. When you get a bone marrow transplant, the kind that I had, they just blast you, get you as close to death as they can. It's surprising how few people die right at that moment, but they are very good at it. [*laughter*] Anyway, in my case I was unconscious—well, not unconscious, but I was so out of it I couldn't even focus on the television screen. For a period of about three weeks, I wrote this poem lying in bed.

I think a great mistake that non-believers make is thinking that what believers want is something abstract: that the fulfillment to longing is an abstraction, it's something that goes on forever, it's the word *eternity*, or it's heaven, it's anything that you can't conceive. In my own experience, in the moments of greatest extremity, what I wanted, what I feared most, was the loss of the particular world right in front of me. And what I wanted most was to be able to apprehend that world in its absoluteness. That's how I understand Christianity: the absolute completely present in the particular.

Love's Last

Love's last urgency is earth
and grief is all gravity

and the long fall always
back to earliest hours

that exists nowhere
but in one's brain.
From the hard-packed

pile of old-mown grass,

from boredom, from pain,
a boy's random slash

unlocks a dark ardor
of angry bees

that link the trees
and block his way home.

I like to hold him holding me,
mystery mastering fear,

so young, standing unstung
under what survives of sky.

I learned too late how to live.
Child, teach me how to die.

When I was a kid—I grew up in West Texas—we found this in a pile of grass. I should have told this before the poem. My brother and I found a pile of grass, and there was a black bee nest in it; we poked it, and eventually *really* poked it, and hundreds of black bees just went all over the yard, just everywhere. Black bees everywhere and I didn't get stung.

Wolfe: The miracle of West Texas. So this longing in some ways is a longing for, as you were putting it, the kind of completion or fulfillment for which we often use the word *happiness*, but a cancer diagnosis is no fun. The reality of life is that it's often full of sorrow, not happiness. And of course a lot of people these days take sorrow or sadness as kind of an excuse for cynicism, or at the extreme, a kind of nihilism, a kind of being half in love with useful death. Can sorrow and happiness somehow be related to each other? Can they feed each other in some sense?

Wiman: Well, I'm certainly familiar with...I mean, I'm a postmodernist poet, and I have inherited the notion that "light writes white." Which is a famous phrase meaning that if everything is light in your life, then you're gonna have a blank page. Light writes white. You gotta have some kind of tension or agony there to produce something. That's the modernist notion about creative artists. The danger of that is that you can fall in love with your treasured and luxurious gloom of choice, as William Wordsworth defined it. Without my loneliness I would be more lonely, says Marianne Moore, so I keep it. I was certainly familiar with that. I needed a way out of it.

I would use the word *joy* instead of *happiness*, simply because in my experience it is possible to feel joy in the midst of suffering. It's not really possible to be happy in the midst of extreme suffering. Joy, I think, surpasses all other emotions, and survives all other emotions. Happiness seems to be a different, different thing.

Wolfe: You mentioned loneliness. It seems to me that so much of modern life reduces us to individuals, and I think it was Whitehead who said something like, "Religion is what we do with our solitude." And yet, as you've written in *My Bright Abyss*, your experience of faith, a longing for the completion, fulfillment, that you found through Christ, has led you away from the cult of loneliness and towards others. How does that play out in your life?

Wiman: Oh, it changed my life. I left an editing job. I was editing a magazine and I left to go to Yale Divinity School, to become a professor. Yale divinity school: I had no divinity training; it was a complete change in my life, and it happened. I mean, you wouldn't believe the set of bizarre circumstances that made it possible. I did it very much because I wanted to put faith at the center of my life, and I wanted to feel a community of believers around me. I think that's very wrong, the notion that religion is what we do with our solitude. I mean, in one way it's right: we all sustain our spiritual lives in solitude. But I'm much more struck by Dietrich Bonhoeffer's notion that Christ is always stronger in our brother's heart than in our own—which seems to be piercingly true. For anyone who feels their faith to be an unstable thing, the thing that stabilizes it is to see it in someone else; to see it credibly enacted in someone else and to feel yourself interacting with that. You know the old Hopkins poem, "Christ plays in ten thousand places / Lovely in limbs, and lovely in eyes not his / To the Father through the features of men's faces."

Wolfe: This longing that points in a direction seems to require a kind of courage, this desire to set out to see, even when the culture may say, "There's nothing there, it's wish fulfillment; it's escapism to believe that there is something that permeates reality beyond the atoms that are interacting in a given space." And I guess that some people have spoken of this risk that people take as the "risk of faith." How do you understand this risk yourself, and how do you deal with the fear that makes you, perhaps, draw back from the leap?

Wiman: We speak in these enormous terms. The poem by Edgar Masters uses these enormous words, *destiny* and *ambition* and *love* and *fear*. We think of the big actions that we're gonna take in our lives to thwart fear, and to act against it. But in my own experience it's actually been the tiniest little ways that you need to act every day, that those immensities get compacted into what you say at the breakfast table. Or the way you treat your kids, or your students. It's actually quite small. And I think the notion of the eternal gets crammed down into our daily lives. It's played out in the most minute, atomic ways, so I don't—you know, how does it play out in me? Badly, I'm sure. I mean, I'm a miserable Christian. I feel like my friend, Fanny Howe, a Catholic woman, whose writings I revere, and whose faith I revere: I was once in one of these situations with her and she said, "You know Chris, I can get up in the morning a believer and go to bed an atheist; happens to me every day." In one way I thought, *Well, that's very depressing*, because if you, who seem amazing to me, are going through that, well then, what hope is there for me? But on the other hand, if she's going through it—well, then there's hope for all of us.

Fanny says that, for her, the form this takes, the form that faith takes, is to risk thinking that we are safe. It's very beautiful, I think: to risk thinking that we are safe. If you're inclined to anxiety, to being overcome by anxiety, to being overcome by your own fears—risk thinking that you're safe. Think about it. And it actually *is* a risk, it feels weird, to think it's all safe.

Wolfe: So...a sense in which faith is both a kind of certainty, and yet also still a journey, still a kind of being on the way. Is that a reasonable definition? I mean, because we encounter in the world people who are absolutely certain in an unhealthy way, and see doubt as the absolute antithesis of what their sense of faith is. But you've spoken of faith as maybe a journey, a kind of having, but at the same time a being on the way.

Wiman: Yeah, I don't feel any sense of certainty at all. And as I say in my book, I don't think I really ever experienced the absence of God until I had lost his presence. I didn't feel it as an agony until I turned to God. I was reading recently Tomas Halik, the Czech priest; very interesting writer. If you haven't read him, he was an underground Catholic priest in Czechoslovakia for years. He talks about the parable of the mustard seed, and you know what the parable of the mustard seed is; Jesus says if you have faith the size of a mustard seed, then you can move mountains. And the way that preachers over the years have used that is, well, if you have this small faith, just a small faith in something, it can grow into a large faith, and you'll be able to do great things with it. But Halik says no, that's exactly wrong. The way to interpret it is: the mustard seed is this tiny thing. You need to think of it as something that's actually been crushed, that's almost nothing; crushed down to this vital, volatile spec. And that's something that can grow.

He says that's what Christianity is in the world today. It's been crushed down to this thing—in his consciousness—and it's crushed down to its essence. Faith can be crushed down to its essence, then it can become something vital and durable, lasting. I was told that he gives these Masses in Prague now, and they are packed with young people, and half of them are unbelievers. He feels that he is called to preach to unbelievers. I often feel that the things that I am writing are addressed to people who are outside of the faith, but looking in. I feel sympathetic to that.

Wolfe: Before we run out of time altogether, I'm a little hungry for some more poetry. Do you have some dog-eared pages where you could maybe favor us with a couple more poems?

Wiman: John Keats, the great poet you quoted earlier, has a letter from 1815 or something. He posits different existences for different things and says there are some things that exist only when we turn our attention to them: they require our attention in order to exist. It has been my experience that faith is like that. I think that I don't have it, I think that God is not real—then I turn my attention to it and I get a response.

When the Time's Toxins
By Christian Wiman

When the time's toxins
have seeped into every cell

and like a salted plot
from which all rain, all green, are gone

I and life are leached
of meaning

Somehow a seed
of belief

sprouts the instant
I acknowledge it:

little weedy hardy would-be
greenness

tugged upward
by light

while deep within
roots like talons

are taking hold again
of this our only earth.

Wiman: Here's another. I grew up in West Texas. Parts of West Texas are fantastic, beautiful. Not where I grew up. [*laughter*] Where I grew up it is completely flat and barren, it's called Snyder. But I wanted to show my wife something there, these tools that my grandfather had that had been in the family forever and were porous from weather. He had hung them on this wall, and one of them was called a raking tooth, and this raking tooth is in this poem.

Here Visible
By Christian Wiman

Here visible
distance

is so much
a part

of things
things

acquire a kind
of space:

I reach
right through

the raking
tooth

that for so long
I've longed

to show you.
I touch

eternity
in your face.

Wiman: All right, here: I went three years without writing poems, and this was before I met my wife and got the diagnosis and all those things conspired to make me right again. And the first poem I wrote—this is a real story—we went to a little church at the end of our street, and for no other reason than it was at the end of our street. I didn't know anything about denominations or anything else; it was a little Protestant UCC church and turned out to be quite a place. And that afternoon I wrote this poem after not having written in three years. It's called "Every Riven Thing." It's the one that gave this book its title. It repeats a line: "God goes, belonging to every riven thing he's made"—and then it changes the punctuation so that the meaning changes. You'll see. *Riven*, by the way, just means torn open, broken.

Every Riven Thing
By Christian Wiman

God goes, belonging to every riven thing he's made
sing his being simply by being
the thing it is:
stone and tree and sky,
man who sees and sings and wonders why

God goes. Belonging, to every riven thing he's made,
means a storm of peace.
Think of the atoms inside the stone.
Think of the man who sits alone
trying to will himself into a stillness where

God goes belonging. To every riven thing he's made
there is given one shade
shaped exactly to the thing itself:
under the tree a darker tree;
under the man the only man to see

God goes belonging to every riven thing. He's made
the things that bring him near,
made the mind that makes him go.
A part of what man knows,

apart from what man knows,

God goes belonging to every riven thing he's made.

Wolfe: It's wonderful, Chris. Well, I think we're just getting warmed up, but we gotta stop. The program goes on, and we're very grateful to you for being here. I know a number of people are going to want to get some books signed after the event, and we'll look forward to that moment. We now have a little bit more to go in this part of the program, but thank you, Chris, very much. [*applause*]

NEW YORK
ENCOUNTER

The Quest to Reduce Extreme Poverty

*Current trends in international development with **Jackie Aldrette**, Managing Director AVSI-USA; **Chris Blattman**, Professor of Political Science, Columbia University; **Joakim Koech**, Principal, Cardinal Otungg High School, Nairobi, Kenya; and **Paolo Carozza** (moderator), Director of the Kellogg Institute at Notre Dame University*

Introduction

What does it mean to promote "development," and where do we place our hope for "success"? The desire to make a positive contribution in the lives of others leads people into careers spanning economics, social services, education, health, and public service, all spurred by a promise of happiness that comes through service toward another. Yet, the world we live in is harsh, and this noble and beautiful desire is often reduced. It is reduced when work is separated from human experience, with its own desire, and the need for happiness is poured into helping others. It is reduced when the ultimate goal is narrowed down to the satisfaction of material needs, or to power. Furthermore, it is reduced when frustration seeps in and one is overwhelmed by a sense of impotence in front of an utterly complex set of interrelated problems. Falling into these traps risks burn-out, disillusionment and lowered expectations.

Carozza: Good morning. It's a privilege to be able to welcome you to the opening discussion of this day at the New York Encounter, and to be here with you. My name is Paolo Carozza and I'm from the University of Notre Dame, where I direct the Kellogg Institute for International Studies. I'm

Saturday, January 16, 2015

here to moderate this discussion today on the "Quest to Reduce Extreme Poverty."

The question of extreme poverty in the world is always present, of course, but has been brought to our attention in recent months and in the last year in particularly prominent and pointed ways in a couple of different contexts. Here in New York, debate and discussion and adoption of the sustainable development goals, for example, set us on a path, gave us an agenda for the coming years on how to address some of these issues globally through international institutions and international cooperation.

Pope Francis, in a similar way, and yet in his inimitably distinct way, also brought to our attention in *Laudato Si'* the big structural questions and causes of not only environmental degradation, the theme which attracted the most public attention to his encyclical, but even more than that, the questions of social exclusion, marginalization, misdevelopment and underdevelopment, and global poverty generally, calling us to a new form of solidarity and social charity.

We've been working on this problem for decades. Of course, with the problem of global poverty—for fifty, sixty, seventy years, at least—there have been international efforts on a systemic basis to try to address them. So, why is it still with us on such a massive scale? Notwithstanding all these decades of work, how much have we really achieved? By some measures, really a lot, actually. The share of people living in poverty globally has never been lower in human history, and by a good measure. In 1981, for example, not that long ago, more than fifty percent of the people in the world lived in absolute poverty. That's down to less than fourteen percent today by the same measure, and poverty today globally is falling more quickly than it ever has before in all of human history.

The world collectively attained the first of the millennium development goals targets—to cut the 1990 poverty rate in half. By 2015, five years early, it was achieved. So at least by measure of income, a great deal has been achieved by anti-poverty efforts in recent years. And beyond income, we could say similar things about global health, decreasing mortality, especially among children and infants and so forth.

And yet, why does the problem still trouble us so much? Well, because there's plenty beyond those measures to indicate to us that the problem of extreme poverty is still massive and acute. Consider a few other basic facts about today's world. Notwithstanding our progress, over 1.3 billion people continue to live in what the World Bank considers to be absolute poverty. If you move the measure of what counts as poverty up to an income of merely $2.50 a day, then the number in poverty increases to about fifty percent of the global population, three billion people. At least eighty percent of all humanity still lives on less than $10 a day. One billion of those people are children. According to UNICEF, twenty-two thousand children per day die because of poverty-related causes. And most of our measures just track income. Again, if we go beyond that to other multi-dimensional measures of poverty that take into account education, health, overall well-being, psychology, spiritual development, the presence of violence—then truly, extreme poverty remains a massive, almost unimaginable global problem. It's not just a sea we are afraid of, but an ocean.

How can we face the problem of global poverty today, and the problem of extreme poverty with any sense of hope, with any sense of possibility that these waters are navigable? That we can do something about it without being oppressed and discouraged by our incapacity to face the basic needs of our brothers and sisters elsewhere in the world? There is, undoubtedly for so many of us, a temptation to just, you could say, "stay home," especially those of us who are—on a daily basis, as my children often like to say—beset and concerned with our "first world problems."

The "first world problems" tag is maybe a useful one to begin our reflection on, because part of the problem, part of the question before us, is whether the problem of extreme poverty is just a problem that is "out there"—elsewhere in the world, a problem of "them"—or is it a problem of "us"? Is it a problem also of our own hearts, our own fears of facing ourselves, the way that we live, the way that we relate to the reality of the world, and to the meaning of things to our everyday experience? In the end, facing it as a reflection about ourselves and not merely about some detached and abstracted conditions somewhere else in the world, the question of our quest to reduce extreme poverty becomes this, an important part. What allows us, still, to face this challenge with energy, with positivity, with hope, with a certainty that there is a good to be sought that is attainable?

To help answer that question, the New York Encounter has assembled a wonderful panel of participants with a range and diversity of experiences to help us reflect on this. I will introduce them all right away so that afterwards we can have much more of an uninterrupted discussion rather than a set of separate presentations.

Intervening first, immediately to my left, will be Joachim Koech, who is the principal of the Cardinal Maurice Otunga High School in Kenya, founded in 2005 and further developed with the help of the Association of Volunteers in International Service, or AVSI. The school aims to develop students' awareness of themselves as human beings with a particular focus on needy students who would not otherwise have access to schooling. Joachim spent sixteen years as a teacher, coach, and deputy principal. He is the former chair of the Cardinal Otunga Charitable Trust and the co-editor of *Reality and Education*. He holds a Masters in Education and Curriculum Studies from the University of Nairobi. Second to my right, Jackie Aldrette is the managing director for AVSI-USA, which is the liaison office for the AVSI Foundation in the United States. Jackie serves as the focal point for U.S. government relations for the entire AVSI network, including local partners present in thirty countries around the world. She has served as the new business program manager for AVSI-USA for the last ten years, supporting its efforts to diversify funding sources and build a foundation of strategic partnerships with U.S. government donor agencies, international financial institutions, foundations, individuals, and universities, including my own.

And third, to the far left is Christian Blattman, Associate Professor of Political Science and International Affairs at Columbia University. Besides being a research fellow with various academic institutes, he leads the Peace and Recovery program at Innovations for Poverty Action, a well-known research institute, as well as the Politics, Institutions and Conflict initiative at Columbia University's Center for Development Economics and Policy. Chris was previously on the faculty at Yale University, and holds a PhD in Economics from the University of California, Berkley and a Master's in Public Administration and International Development from Harvard's

Kennedy School of Government.

As you can see, we have a range of experiences here. Joachim works directly with students in his native Nairobi. Jackie brings to us a perspective informed by years working with a national development NGO. And Chris Blattman, from the world of academics, perhaps works in the broadest way on the intellectual and research questions that emerge from all of this work. So we'll begin with Joachim. Joachim, can you tell us a little bit about what you do, and more importantly, why you do it, and what we can learn from it?

Koech: Thank you, Paolo. Good morning, everyone. I'm happy to be here with you. It is my first time in America, and so my first time in New York. I never expected to be here. But now I am here, and this is interesting because the journey that has happened in my life brought me here. If I were to imagine back several years ago, I could not think that I could be here, talking about my life, talking about the work that I am doing, because when I finished college, I trained as a teacher; but after college I didn't want to teach. I thought it was too little; I wanted to be rich. [*laughter*] I wanted to be a businessman, I wanted to make money. And therefore, that's what I did. I went out after college and I started to do some work as an entrepreneur for two years. Now, let's think about this—this was the project that I had: how to make a good transport business. In Kenya, we have small minibuses of fourteen to eighteen, and with some money, some contributions, I bought one, and this was a business I started. I was imagining myself in several years owning a fleet of this kind of bus. Incidentally, one day, the principal of my high school met me on the road, and he asked, "Please help me, I need a teacher of Swahili! My teacher has been transferred. Can you stand in for him?" So, I said, "Okay. Maybe in the morning, when I'm free, maybe in the morning for two hours"—and this is what happened. I went there for two hours, and now I'm here. [*laughter*]

This, among other things, when I put them together, showed me what it really means, the path of life. We have an imagining of the path, and we have some instances of life that help us to discover this path that is useful for us, perhaps unexpectedly. Now, he's asking me a big question: What am I developing in the school? But at the same time, when we teach, I think this happens. Now, when I went back to school, I did not know really what I wanted to tell the students. I did not know what I wanted to teach them. This is why, in the first place, I was not comfortable to go. And, after working in the public school, I did very well, because in a few years I was promoted to deputy principal in a big school, because I was very tough with the students, very strict. They thought this is the way to teach them. To be tough, to be disciplined, this is what the parents also liked, this is why they promoted me very fast. [*laughter*]

Afterwards, I went to Nairobi. I was living there, outside, three-hundred kilometers from the capital city. I went to do a masters there and I met some friends. During this time, I went to teach in a very good school, a very good Catholic school. At that time also, I met some friends, one named Father Voladio, one named Paulo Sana, and one named Stefano Mancini: my friends who were teachers in other schools. They were reading a book called *The Risk of Education*. I met them because my wife was working with them—that's how I met these friends of mine.

It was very interesting, because next time, when I was teaching in another school, it was just part-time, and I asked why sometimes poverty remains, why things don't change. It really disturbed me, and I think this is connected to the way someone looks at you, the way someone treats you, the way someone takes care of you. Already it gives an expression. This school, it was a very good school, but I only tell this story because it was really what changed my position about teaching. It was a very well-made school, very good buildings. But, what was missing were the toilets. The toilets were outside the classrooms, without doors and without lights. So imagine the students that used these in the evening when it was dark. You have to go to a toilet outside the building. And in the morning, they were very dark. Some of the students had to watch this. I was very uncomfortable with this.

So I went, we spoke with my friends, because we were meeting these teachers—Father Voladio, Paulo Sana, and other people—and I was saying, "There is something that I am a bit uncomfortable with about the school. We are doing well, but there is something that is really—the students have to go to this toilet that is dark, very dark, and then also keep in mind that it's a budding school, four hundred students. And in the evening, they have to use these toilets, maybe six of them, without the doors. The one who is waiting for you...can you imagine? People are waiting outside there. So we asked, What is missing in this? What is missing in this good school? Because it was a good school, it was doing very well, the building was really well-done. It had been erected by missionaries, so this provoked me a lot.

My friends were saying, "Is it possible to find a place where we can look at these students in a different way?" This was a question we started to think about. And it happened: Otunga School was born from this, the bad luck that we were having. Is it possible to find a place where we can really dialogue about what it means to teach, to educate, to take care of the students? We didn't have anything. But we spoke with AVSI, and some friends were ready to support us, and we started the school. It's been a great help for me to understand why people don't change. They don't change because sometimes it's how we look at them. You can have very nice things, but that doesn't matter, because it's not total change, it's not total awareness, and so I'm not changed completely. My way of looking at reality, my way of looking at the other person, is not changed. And I'm grateful that I'm here, and that I met these friends of mine, that they told me about Giussani and his concern about education and his concern about the young people. The first day we opened the school, when we opened the gate of the school, the parents came—we have children from able families, but a number of children come from very poor backgrounds. So on the first day when we opened the gate to the school, some parents of these children when they arrived at the gates—the school was made very well, it was clean—when they reached the gate of the school, some of them removed their shoes. *You cannot step on this because it is very clean.* And then when they walked around, some of the mothers cried, and they were asking, "Now you are sure this is for my son?" Yes. "Well, why? We don't even pay a single shilling, so why would you build something like this for him?"

This became something else for me, because from that moment I knew that this mother had taught me something, that sometimes we take things for granted. Her reaction was, "We don't deserve it, but we are already given it. We don't deserve it, but we already have something in front of us that is beautiful." So I learned from her. And staying with my students became—this is the point—I want them when they arrive in school to have the feeling that their lives are great, I want them to perceive it when they enter the gate. That their lives are great and the consequence of this awareness, of this dialogue among us, the teachers, and the students, is because with the teachers we decided to talk about what it all means.

I'd like to mention a friend of Father Giussani named Piccinini. Father Giussani was asking him, "So how do you know that you love your children?" And Piccinini responds, "In the evening when I arrive home, because I don't want to disturb them, I tip-toe to their bedroom, kiss each one of them, and it feels good afterwards when I see all of them asleep." Father Giussani says, "But that is not enough. Because if you love them very much, then the question that will come is, 'But will happen to them? What is their destiny?'" This question has also become my question when I go to school. When I see the kids coming to school, I ask myself, "What will happen to them?"

These questions have become useful for us as teachers, and the students start to grow, to take their lives seriously. But above all, I'm seeing that I was the first one who started to change. The way I look at myself, the way I look at the walk, the way I look at my children. And then, the teachers also; and the students. We have had very good results. This is not because I'm very strict or very—you see how it happens. Before, it was very good results, but very demanding. Now, the results are coming a in different way: out of a gratitude, out of an awareness that somebody wants to struggle, they want to make a difference, they want to keep the school clean, they want to take care of their children, their families. And teachers now, they want more. There is a teacher who wanted to transfer, but he came and told me, "I can't. When I think about all the work you are doing here, how it has been useful for me and my children, I would like to give more time, and I would like to make these children also do well."

Our students have grown for this reason. I could give you many, many reasons, but I think at the core of the change is the hope that has pushed me. I decided that this is really what I want to express because I said it to take care of myself. And I wanted to express this to my students. I see this happening, and this is my hope, because I see that I'm growing even now. I'm growing every day and my students are growing, and our teachers are growing, and it makes a big difference. In fact, I always say that even if everything goes wrong, I'm certain of this fact: something has happened that has made me different and changed. And I expressed this to my students. [*applause*]

Aldrette: Well, my story is quite different from Joachim's, and my daily work as well. As Paolo mentioned, I work at AVSI-USA, which is the U.S. branch of this international, non-profit organization, AVSI, which was started in the early 1970s by some people of the movement Communion and Liberation.

My daily work is primarily in four different areas. First, we try to find opportunities for funding, from US government agencies, AVSI projects in Africa and Latin America, which requires a lot of effort and a lot of networking.

Secondly, we raise money from individuals to enable AVSI to respond to crises and emergencies around the world where we're able to. We also work with foundations, which is a really important part of our job, because it allows us to respond to really concrete needs with our partner organizations on the ground, and to fill in some gaps from what we're able to fundraise from individuals and from other donors, to respond to concrete needs such as building a classroom, or putting books in libraries, that kind of thing.

We also connect the world of AVSI, this network of AVSI, and all of our partners with universities, with students interested in doing internships. We try to do some research into our work in order to understand it better. This is the kind of thing we're involved with on a daily basis.

How did I get into this? I'd like to share just a little bit of my story and the growth that I've had to go through to stay in front of this desire, as Paolo launched the question to us.

I come from a background that's probably familiar to most of us, many of you: a middle-class American family, growing up with a good education, lots of opportunities. As I was getting through my college years, I had basically two main questions driving me. One was how I could reconcile my life, everything that I'd been given, with what I had seen, the poverty and the suffering, the inequality of opportunity I had seen around the world in my travels. This is the big question for me, and one that I felt could easily be tamped down, pushed away, and allow me to just kind of go on with life as if the problem didn't exist. But I knew that I didn't really want to do that, I really wanted to take it seriously.

The other question that was really burning in me at that time, around the year 2000, with everyone talking about globalization and these big economic forces connecting the world, creating opportunities and yet putting in our face the stark contrasts in terms of how we live here in the U.S. and the life of so many people around the world—the intuition in front of that was that globalization must have something to offer the world's poor, and even the poor in our own countries. Why can't we figure out some ways of tapping into all this power, all this opportunity, all this economic excess? And somehow address suffering, address poverty. With these questions I decided to pursue an international career, and when I discovered that there was this whole field of international organizations engaged right here, right there in that intersection, it was like a big *A-ha!* moment. This is an amazing thing, right? I'm gonna be paid, potentially, to work for an organization that serves the poor—fantastic! That meets all my needs. And then when I came across AVSI, again it was an amazing opportunity for me, because not only was it a chance to discover what it means to work on behalf of the poor of the world, and tap into some of the resources of the U.S. and the developed countries on behalf of communities around the world, but to do so within a Catholic perspective, within a perspective that I'm also serving the Church.

On a certain level, I have an amazing job. I'm very happy with that, and it's an opportunity to address the question of what we can do to help the poor in a really concrete way. But the journey that I've been on has been interesting, because to stay in front of that is not automatic and is not simple. I'm really helped by an encounter and a judgment that I received at the beginning of my time with AVSI, from my very dear colleague, Ezio, who has, as many of you know, dedicated most of his professional life to working with AVSI. Early in my time with AVSI, we were sitting around and talking with some other people about why we do this work, and he put it this way: he said, "We don't do this work because we have something to offer someone else; we don't have a solution to someone else's problems. Instead, we do this work because we have received something. We do this work because we have been loved." Maybe the difference is a little bit subtle. At first I thought I understood it, but it's been a work for me to really understand what it means. I'm really grateful for it because, in those moments in which I don't have clarity about why I'm doing this work, sometimes even the tasks can seem mundane, since most of my day is spent with a computer, a budget, with a project proposal—and not embracing the poor in a physical, concrete way. I have to go back to that question, and to that starting point and say, Okay, is this about me? Is this about what I can do? Is this about what I can produce? Or is my interest in the life of someone I don't know who's far away? Does that come from somewhere else? Right? And does my response to that come from a really deep sense of my own belonging and the fact that I've met something that gives my life meaning? So I would say that some of the risks, some of the reductions that I fall into in approaching this work is, on one level, a kind of intellectualism. You know, you can think about poverty in a very academic, intellectual kind of way, and forget the human person that you're actually working for, and forget that the human person is also a free being. We have to resist the temptation to think about solutions to poverty that are systems and policies that are then going to "solve problems."

I struggle with a romantic idea of what it means to serve the poor, in the sense that sometimes my struggle is from the heart, the desire to embrace, to be close to the people I believe I am serving. Then again, I think that it's a struggle that many of us might face in other types of work as well, putting ourselves at the center of what we're doing. Getting caught up in your results as the definition of how well you're working, right? What helps me stay in front of the big desire that started everything, that got me here, is going back to that: it's being really open to the question of what it is I hope for my life, what I hope to do with my work. I've learned over time that this question needs to be also really rooted in reality, in objective work and circumstances that I've been given.

I just want to share one little story that was really useful for me, a moment of growth for me. About a year, year-and-a-half ago, I was feeling a kind of dissatisfaction with work, feeling like I was far away from what I really wanted to be doing. Far away, maybe, from the core of what AVSI does every day. I was really frustrated with an office job. At the same time, I was planning a mission to Haiti. In the back of my mind, one of the reasons I was going to Haiti was to reconnect. I really thought that I was going to reconnect with the poor there, and see faces that would help me be more inspired. I went, and I did encounter and meet with a number of our beneficiaries, the community, the women we work with, and these were beautiful interactions. And yet, in a few days you can only interact so much, and I felt I couldn't even really get to know them. The week was spent mostly with my colleagues, both the international staff who were there, and the local staff. I was really struck by the intensity of our relationship and the way in which they stay in front of the poor that they have been with on a daily basis. I was also struck by the way I was with my colleagues, because I could see a change in me and the way that I was asking them questions, helping them to probe also their experience. Asking them why they were doing this work? What kept them going? And too, just helping them to be open to the reality that they were living in.

I came back with this sense of being so honored to work for my staff, our staff. It really helped me in this journey of understanding my desire. But what does it mean within the concrete job that I've been given, which maybe doesn't match up with this romantic idea that I had, but that's also very fulfilling? That's what I think is really useful for everybody: the desires we have are big, but they have to be in dialogue with reality. There's a great amount of fulfillment when it's clear to us that we're working and responding, not just to some far-off idea but to a presence and something that's been asked of me here and now. [*applause*]

Blattman: So, I wanted to be a historian, right? And maybe twelve or fifteen years ago I spent a lot of my time three levels underground in the university library, collecting statistics on developing countries. Then twelve years ago I found myself in a town called Kitgum in northern Uganda, where there was a war going on, just the dying days of a twenty-year war, two million people displaced. I'd gone there for the noblest of reasons—I'd followed a woman. [*laughter*] She was a psychologist, she worked with AVSI, and she was studying how to help people, especially children and women, recover from war, and her passion became my passion. I began studying the long-term effects of war on children, on youth, and on what recovery might look like and what it really meant to recover from really what was one of the most disastrous and traumatizing events in human history.

It felt very hopeless at the beginning. The war ended shortly after I started working, and people had lost everything. This was a relatively prosperous corner of Africa; there were more cattle than people at one point. People had homes and farms, and all of that was gone. People had been displaced into camps, they'd lost everything, and they had just returned home to desolate fields and houses that had crumbled and no livestock whatsoever. AVSI had a very provocative approach. A very controversial approach. One that I did not initially believe would work. They would go to these little villages of maybe a hundred households, who had just returned to their land, and they would find the fifteen poorest households, usually women, in what was already one of the poorest places on the planet. Maybe the poorest place on the planet. Then, they gave them cash. They gave them $150 to help them start a business, which might be to go to the market in the capital, or the local capital, and bring back and sell oil or matches or maybe sell some vegetables, or maybe to buy some livestock. They would give them a little bit of training and a little bit of advising, but really these women—who in many cases had no education, who had really nothing and no experience, some of them had lived the previous eight years in a displacement camp with no job at all, with no activity whatsoever—these women were supposed to be entrepreneurs and grow rich.

Partly in hope and partly in disbelief, we started a study. We started following these women over several years. We looked at those who received the program in the first year—we could only serve so many programs, this was intensive, a lot of money to raise. Most donors would say, This is crazy, we're not going to give the poorest people in the world a cash hand-out; they're not going to be business people. They'll drink it, or they'll waste it, they'll make bad decisions, and if they sell something they'll sell the same thing that those five other people are selling and nobody will make any money. What do they know?

We followed them, and we followed women who were going to receive it down the road as well, and after a year or two we could look at the impact of AVSI's idea by contrasting these two groups—those who had received it, and those who were about to receive it. What we saw was astonishing. We saw that previously these women might have earned not even a dollar a day, maybe a few dollars a week. Then they'd started small businesses. They were spending five or ten hours a week tending the livestock and selling the product, and selling their goods and becoming, basically, traders. They made great decisions. Even though they were selling the same five junky things that everybody else was selling, somehow this was actually a shockingly profitable activity. "Shockingly profitable" in the sense that, before, they made four or five dollars a week, and now, they made ten dollars a week. This may not sound like a whole lot, but it's in some sense what it means to end extreme poverty. This is the difference between eating once a day and twice a day—and eating twice a day is a big deal. It wasn't the solution, right? They weren't off earning a wage in a job and sending their children to university, but they were eating twice a day instead of once a day.

We challenged AVSI. We said, "Your model is wonderful, it seems to be working; but you can only help a thousand people at a time, because you're doing a lot of training, a lot of advising, there's a lot of hand holding. It takes a lot of time. You can't help ten thousand people like this, you can't help a hundred thousand, you can't help a hundred million, and that's what it means to end extreme poverty." We told them that the women hadn't wasted the money, that they'd made good decisions. Maybe it's because AVSI helped them, but maybe they can do this on their own. When they helped the second group of women, the ones we'd been comparing them to, we challenged AVSI and said, "What if you just give some of them the money and a day or two of training, and see whether they can do this on their own?" Most organizations wouldn't do that. It was a brave step, and the women who received some help, of course they did a little bit better. But not so much better that it justified spending more money than the cash grant itself on helping them sustain their business. The women who received this helping hand, this cash, started successful businesses, they doubled their income, they ate twice a day instead of once a day, their children were more likely to go to school and were healthier. I think that what this shows is that the problem of ending poverty is maybe one of the slowest and most complex and most difficult things in the world. Getting people to have the opportunity to send their children to college and to earn large incomes and have big businesses will be very, very slow, and it will happen. But ending *extreme* poverty may be a little bit simpler: helping people go from eating once a day to eating twice a day and maybe then, eventually, to eating three times a day. This might be a little more straightforward, and it may require a great deal of humility, it might require a great deal more trust and faith in the poor, whom we're often very quick to write off as likely to make bad decisions, or are incapable of knowing what's best, or wasting or drinking away or otherwise really requiring us to walk them through the process of development. I don't think the stereotypes are true. I think it requires humility, a willingness to put our trust in these people, and give them, in this case, the things they need.

This led me, in my research career, to start identifying daring solutions like this one, and try to study them, try to understand how it relates to poverty. I've done things that a dozen other people have done, and have shown this same result. Giving people cash—or cattle, or some form of capital—shows very, very similar results around the world. People lurch forward.

You asked why we're hopeful. The reason I'm hopeful about ending extreme poverty is because I think there are basic ingredients that are not so complicated, but that require us to be a great deal less paternalistic and a great deal more humble towards those less fortunate.

Carozza: Thank you. [*applause*] Thanks to all three of you. We do have some time to engage in follow-up on these presentations, and put them into conversation with one another a little bit.

One question I would like to ask all three of you is this: it struck me that from very different sets of experiences and perspectives, and in different ways, all of you in one way or another emphasized two interrelated things. One is the absence, or the impossibility, almost, of formulaic solutions to the problem: there's a formula, you plug it in, and if we do this, we solve poverty. A completely dehumanized kind of system. And reciprocally, related to that, is the presence and need to come to terms with the problem of human freedom; in particular, the risks that freedom entails. We're setting out in this area, and all of you talked about having to take risks, and the uncertainty necessarily introduced into that by dealing with people in their freedom.

For a lot of us, that's a source of fear. We want solutions that are certain, we want solutions that are formulaic, we want systems that we can put in place, so that we can give our money to them and that's going to solve the problem: no more child mortality in the world. So could you say a little bit more about where you think the question of freedom and the associated risk it entails fits into your work? How do you see it? How do you address it? Why is it important, and what can we learn about taking it into account from the perspective of the work that you do? Who'd like to begin?

Aldrette: An idea comes to mind that I think is connected to your question and to something that Chris said. Chris put the challenge of scale in front of us, right? The scale of poverty is big, and maybe what we're doing is on such a small scale that you have to ask yourself: Is this the best use of resources to make a dent in the problem? To reach any kind of scale?

Another big, challenging question that we want to talk about is sustainability. Is what we're doing something that can be sustained over time? Or are we always going to be needed? Like Chris also mentioned—the idea of paternalism. Are we always going to be needed there, providing some input? I bring up this question of sustainability and whether our results are lasting, because I see a connection with risk and freedom, in the sense that what we've learned is that the best bet that we can make with our investment, with our money, with our resources and our time are in those people, and in those organizations that have come up from the communities themselves to answer a need they have identified, and that they have the energy and the courage to address. I feel this is risky in the sense that we as an organization aren't going to define the solution and have control over some package that we deliver, that we can control how it's delivered. Instead, we want to bet on freedom and the desire and the intelligence and conviction of people themselves. Our method, then, becomes one of observing what's happening in the places where we are, and seeing where things are growing, and trying to put our efforts there. It's sometimes unsatisfying, because where we can serve and help one school, like Otunga School where Joachim is, there are many other very worthy schools out there that also need help and we cannot reach them. It's true. The problem of scale for us is a really good challenge and a dramatic one. But if we can invest in a few places that then can become examples for their community, we think that that's an impact that will last much longer than when we're around or when our money is being used.

Carozza: Anyone else?

Koech: In school, I see the risk that really makes a difference is if a student or even a teacher or the people that we work with—feel it. An example. The person who cleans the school compound, he does it very well. And I don't follow him to tell him to do this or that, but he knows that I really trust him, he knows that I bet on him. So on a Friday evening he says, "I have a plan for tomorrow," and so on, "I'm going to do"... you know. Then when we arrive on Monday morning I see what he has done. He's done a very good job. I use it as an example for the students: "Do you see how this guy is working? Do you see how he takes care of everything?" Yes.

Sometimes the teachers have lots of doubts, because someone is making mistakes, because someone is not progressing. But I say, when they come to school, what are they looking for? What is everyone looking for, even in an unconscious [way]? We're looking for something good for our lives. When we wake up in the morning there is a good that we are looking for. Sometimes it's not very clear. Therefore if I encounter someone who trusts me as this good starts to come out, but then that someone doubts me, then this good will never, never be expressed, and will never change me. Not at the concrete level of the human person. I can tell you are stupid, or I can tell you now you can make me sick, but it's possible to grow; you can change. I trust in this. And someone perceives this. If there is someone in front of you who helps you to regain confidence about life, about meaning, it makes a big difference. And I think this is for me an example of development, because if someone gains confidence he can face life, he can struggle, he can make a lot of changes. But it depends a lot on how I look at. This is why I was using the example of the guy, because one of my friends told me, "There's a lack in this school." Why? "Because there is a way of looking at a person that is not complete." So you give them a piece of good building, but there's a way of looking at this person that reduces even the beautiful building.

Carozza: Chris, moving to a different area, your work in particular is necessarily—and quite amazingly—about measurement. Measurement, in one way or another, represents one of our recent years' most significant and dramatic changes in the way we work in development. The sophistication of our capacity to measure, the tools that are available, and the omnipresence of efforts to measure. Given that this is your daily fare and your currency and your contribution, I wonder if you could share with us your thoughts on the uses and value of measurement, as it relates to what we're talking about. Also, the potential limitations of measurement. I mean, where does it fall short? We live in a society in an era that is obsessed with measuring everything, and reducing everything to measurement; where might this also impede or blind us to some of the things that are necessary for addressing extreme poverty in a comprehensive way?

Blattman: AVSI is a small faith-based organization. I like to say that the U.S. government and the World Bank and the organizations that pour billions into poor countries are also faith-based organizations, but it's a different kind of faith. It's a faith that they're doing works, and it's a faith that's been based on very little introspection. One of the things that's happened in the last fifteen years is a push to actually see which of our activities actually make an impact. We fund job training programs, we support the growth of micro-finance institutions, we put in girls' scholarships and textbooks and deworming medicine. All of these things happen over and over and over again, some of which probably work really well and maybe all of them work, and maybe none of them work, and maybe we can be more effective. I think one of the revolutions that's happened through measurement in the last fifteen years is the discovery that some of these things have no impact on poverty at all. Vocational skills training programs have almost no impact on poverty at all. As a society, we spend maybe a hundred million dollars every six months on that. No impact at all. Micro-finance does many wonderful things, but it has close to zero impact on income and poverty despite many peoples' hopes and aspirations and very plausible beliefs. We've learned some very profound things about projects we thought will work, but don't.

And then we've found some things—like what AVSI did—that sound crazy but work really well. Another example is very simple, short, cognitive behavior therapy for street youth. Something I've worked on in war-affected societies, the hardest-core criminals in society. Whether this is inner-city Chicago or inner-city Liberia and Monrovia, it dropped crime levels by half after a very cheap, eight-week course of group therapy with some of their peers. There are other approaches, other ways we can learn, but I think we're just starting.

Carozza: Thank you. There are so many other questions to ask, but we don't have a lot of time. I'll limit myself to just one more for each of you. One of the beautiful things about the New York Encounter is how many young people come here from around the country, from around the world. All of you, each of you, has years of experience in your fields, addressing this problem, and each of you talked about how, at an early stage, you were motivated by a certain kind of youthful idealism and even, perhaps, of a romantic stripe at a certain point. What would you say in just a minute or two, to all of the young people here and all of the young people who have an idealism, to try and use their lives to address the problems of extreme poverty in the world? What advice would you give them? Where to begin, and how to think about what their own role in this should be?

Koech: The first thing that made the difference for me in all my struggles, was when somebody told me it's possible to find the truth, it's possible to meet the truth, to find the way. My struggle was: What is the use of my life? Before, there was no need to struggle because this thing was not there. But the most surprising thing was when somebody said, "Imagine today, where you are, that you meet someone who tells you this is the way, the truth, and the life." And I was very surprised, because I was looking for this but I'd never thought it possible. Imagine someone telling you now that this way is the truth, this life. This is exactly what I'm looking for. [*Applause*] This is why I'm here. I don't have fear because I discovered that this way is the truth, this life, and that I'm not alone. I can face life because I discover I'm not alone and I have someone to ask, someone to help me make a decision, even. For example, I'm going to New York. I call a friend of mine, and I ask, "What do you think this is, what are the signs?" If they refuse you the visa, he said, then of course you can't go. So I went to apply for the visa and they didn't ask me any questions. They didn't even ask me for an invitation letter. It was a clear sign that I was to come here and be part of this. As you grow, as you move, you find this, that you are not alone, there's someone you can ask. You fear because your mission is sometimes small, and that is what happened to me. My mission was small, and therefore sometimes I feared. But now I'm so free because it's not my mission. It's no longer my mission. It's someone else's, and I'm free. I can take a risk, and this is the best thing that can happen. It is possible to find someone that you can trust, and with whom you can trust your life, your questions, all the doubts, all the joys, and everything. [*applause*]

Blattman: I guess the only thing I'll add is this: continuing with the theme of humility, I would go to a place and would get to know a place, and would get to understand the situation. I would go with questions, not answers. And I would stick with questions, not answers, for a very long time. This is incompatible sometimes with youthful idealism, but, it's truly important. [*applause*]

Aldrette: I would add that for the young person it's important to really be attentive to your interests, to your whole, all of yourself, and to keep open the questions that you have, not to be afraid of them and to seek out people who help you address the questions of your vocation, of the life path that has been set out for you and to keep that as a constant journey that you're on. I would also mention the importance of relationships. We see over and over again that poverty isn't just a material thing. If we want to make a difference, it comes down really to relationships, and this is something that we can all pay attention to and practice in our lives: how we look at one another, how we treat one another. Whether you end up in a direct confrontation with poverty or not is something that changes the world. [*applause*]

Carozza: I think it's good that we end with so many open questions to keep alive, even though we can't address them right now for lack of time, given all of the other wonderful events we have on the program for the Encounter today. I'd like to thank AVSI in general for helping make this panel possible, and putting so much behind getting all of us here and for all the work that has inspired this discussion. You can learn and see a lot more about AVSI if you go upstairs to the exhibit on the second floor. It's one of the exhibits of the Encounter devoted to AVSI and AVSI's work. I encourage you to see it. And other than that, it only remains for us to thank our panelists one more time. [*applause*]

NEW YORK

WIDMER

ALBIN

Doing Business in Uncharted Waters

A dialogue on leading companies unafraid to explores new business horizons with ***Nancy Albin****, Co-founder of Los Angeles Habilitation House;* ***Andreas Widmer****, Director of the Entrepreneurship Programs, Catholic University of America; and* ***Anujeet Sareen****, Portfolio Manager at Brandywine Global Investment Management.*

Introduction

"Work is an expression of being. This awareness is a breath of fresh air for the worker who toils in his workplace for eight hours and for the entrepreneur working hard to develop his business. But our being—that which the Bible calls 'heart' and is made of courage, tenacity, cleverness, hard work—is thirst for truth and happiness. There are no works, from the humble one of the housewife to the brilliant one of the designer that can escape this reference and this search for a complete satisfaction and human fulfillment...

Desire is the spark with which an engine gets started. Every human action is born from this phenomenon, from this dynamism which constitutes man. It's desire that turns on 'man's engine.' As a consequence, he starts looking for bread and water, for work, for a woman; he looks for a more comfortable armchair and a better house. He starts getting interested in the fact that some people have more than others, he looks at the fact that some people are treated in a certain way and he's not, precisely because of the growing and maturing of these inspirations he has within himself."
(Msgr. Luigi Giussani, *Notes from a talk to the General Assembly of the members of* Compagnia delle Opere, 1987)

Saturday, January 16, 2016

Why does anyone decide to undertake the risk of starting a company, since the outcome is so unpredictable? What gives the courage to develop new business models and to enter unexplored entrepreneurial territories?

Sareen: Welcome, everyone. Before starting, I would like to thank the Work Center for helping organize this event. The Work Center is a volunteer association of workers who strive to accompany people in the challenging journey of seeking a job, or considering a change in career path. Their mission statement reads as follows: "Together we try to unveil the real needs at the basis of the job search and the positive aspects of this journey. We offer help in reviewing and editing resumes, preparing job seekers for interviews, encouraging them when difficulties seem to prevail, and building contacts starting from our own professional networks. We also organize events in a broad range of topics, related to the nature and meaning of work in light of the Christian Event. You can learn more by visiting our website at www.workcenter.org." And I would just emphasize that all the services at the Work Center are freely offered.

So, the event at hand: "Doing Business in Uncharted Waters." I work for an investment company in Boston. We're in the business of investing our clients' money around the world in the most successful businesses we can find, the most profitable businesses we can find. But, over the last ten years, we find that our clients are increasingly asking us about what's the ESG score of the companies we invest in. ESG stands for Environment, Social, and Governance. Environment: Are these companies helping to preserve the environment or are they doing the opposite? Social: How are they treating their employees, are they selling products of integrity, and how are they impacting the communities in which they operate? Governance: How are their executives compensated, how are they treating the shareholders and employees? Also, is there a sense of transparency and disclosure?

There's some preliminary evidence that companies that take some of these issues seriously do better. Now maybe that's because they avoid litigation, maybe it's because customers want to support these companies in some of the things that they're doing, or maybe they are more sustainable businesses when they consider some of these factors and what they do. I don't think that's necessarily the most interesting aspect of this. What's interesting to me is that in the ten years since the financial crisis, there is a different question being asked. What is the business of business? What does business serve? Who does it serve?

I'm really excited today because I think we have two speakers with us who can help us go a lot deeper into these questions. To my left is Nancy Albin. Nancy is co-founder of The Los Angeles Habilitation House, or LAHH. She is providing vision, management, and leadership in the major corporate economic strategies, objectives, and policies overseeing LAHH, and accounting, budgeting, tax, treasury, administrative functions and automation efforts. Nancy has over nine years of combined experience in corporate balance sheet audits with a Big Four accounting firm, and financial budgeting, forecasting, and analysis with a Fortune 500 company that is a leader in family entertainment.

To my right is Andreas Widmer. Andreas is a director of entrepreneurship programs at the Catholic University of America and president of the Carpenter's Fund. He was previously co-founder of the Seven Fund, a philanthropic organization run by entrepreneurs who invested in original research, books, and films to further enterprise solutions to poverty. He's the author of *The Pope & The CEO: Pope John Paul II's Leadership Lessons to a Young Swiss Guard*, a book exploring leadership lessons learned by a Swiss guard protecting Pope John Paul II, and refined during his career as a successful business executive. He's a frequent speaker around the world, on issues related to business ethics, entrepreneurship, business leadership, productivity, and the challenges of executive management.

Welcome to you both. [*applause*] I think maybe the place to start is with the theme of the New York Encounter, which is "Longing for the Sea and Yet Not Afraid." I thought maybe we can start with you, Nancy, and really focus on the point about longing. You have this job at Walt Disney, 2000-2008, sounds like a pretty good job, sounds like a job you like—then something changes. Something changes in terms of what you want to be doing and what attracts you, and I was hoping that you could talk more about that.

Albin: Sure, absolutely. I like the question your customers are asking after the crisis, because after the tsunami that hit Sri Lanka—I don't know how many of you remember that, but for me the question about work changed after I saw the destruction in Sri Lanka. And I didn't even know anyone who died in that event. I started to ask myself some very important questions: What am I doing with my time, my talents, and my education? Questions full of hope, possibility. I'd lost friends in 9/11, which was much more personal, but this question wasn't, "Oh my gosh, the world is in a moment of destruction or a moment of end," but it was a beginning. Because I understood that the value of what you do at your workplace is so much more than just the task, or the supervisor's approval, or the praise that you may receive. I can't do many things, and I'm not interested in everything. The interest that I had felt very personal and specific to me, and I shared it with my very good friend, Guido Piccarolo, a discussion and dialogue that we continue to have to this day, which is one of the best things to blossom—a fruit—from this question. I would say we've deepened that initial longing and that initial attraction of what my specific interest is, my work, my energy that I'm putting to my task today. The meaning of that and the depth of that has become more a point of departure day after day.

Sareen: Thank you. So maybe the same question for you, Andreas. I know in your background you've been an entrepreneur of a technology company, you've been a philanthropist, now you're a professor who teaches about entrepreneurship, and before all that, you were in the Swiss Guard. So there's clearly a sense of searching, of longing for something. Can you talk to us about that?

Widmer: My life is a big ol' search, right? People are always surprised. I didn't go into the Swiss Guard because of any religious piety or religious belief. You know, as the Swiss, you have this privilege to go into the Swiss Guard, but really, you only have to be Catholic, like, baptized and confirmed and that's as high as you have to jump. It's a bit more strenuous on the physical side, and of course they like big guys like me. I joined because I'm the youngest of six in my family. I grew up in the middle of nowhere in Switzerland, my village has four hundred people in it, you can't even find it on a map. And I really struggled in finding who I am. You know, if you're the youngest, all your older siblings, even if they're terrible at something, they're still better than you. [*laughter*] You know? And so I really struggled. I had a tough time in school, and I just didn't know who I was and what life was all about. I started, basically, trying to prove myself. I was sort of a tough little guy, ya know? I excelled in military and eventually went into this. When I heard that I could be a bodyguard, I could be trained to be a bodyguard, and be paid for that, I'm like, Okay, that's me, that's what I'm going to do. And I did this to impress others. The fact that I had to protect the pope didn't really mean anything to me. And then I met John Paul. Actually, I met him right when I started to find out that, now that I've impressed others by being a Swiss Guard, I was very empty. I started to accuse myself of being a total idiot, of having gone to a foreign country for nothing. You know, Italy is not an easy country to live in as a Swiss person, let me tell you. [*laughter*] I tried to cross the street in Italy but couldn't. [*laughter*] Those Italians are color-blind.

I actually had a crisis where it all came to a head: "You've looked for this happiness and for what makes you happy, and here you are, miserable as ever." It happened that I was on duty one night—actually it was Christmas evening and I just totally lost it, and I cried my eyes out. You know, many posts in the Vatican where you work as a Swiss Guard you're on your own, you're off in some room up in the Vatican palace or something and nobody's there, especially during the night. But that night, suddenly John Paul comes out, and I'm crying, and he noticed. He ministered to me in a very profound way, not telling me what to do, but in reaching out to me as a human person. Not as the pope, but as one man to another, telling me that he would pray for me. And that was the beginning of the change of my life. I still get goose bumps now; when somebody reaches out to you, and you're totally alone, and you totally think that you're worthless, and that your life is worthless, that really makes a difference, so much so that I then looked at him and said, "Wow, whatever you have, that's what I want; I want to live like that." And then, instead of taking this on himself, he pointed to Christ and said, "What I have, you can have." Then, by the grace of God, I received the gift of faith. I know you want to do a sort of bookend and say that everything was fine after that, but no, I continued to be an idiot. Winning it, losing it—living in the grace, I want to say, and then not. My life is one step forward, three steps back. But the theme of it has always been this longing. I think it comes out of this idea of longing for acceptance, for peace, for what they said yesterday, that it's okay to take the plunge into the faith, that it's going to be okay. Because I kept thinking that I had to prove something to somebody. John Paul showed me that I actually don't, that my dignity doesn't come from what I do, it comes from who I am.

Sareen: Thank you. Nancy, let's go back again to the title, "Longing for the Sea, Yet Not Afraid." There's an element of risk in that quote, and I'm really struck by the fact that, again, you've got this really good job at Walt Disney, it's 2008, the world's falling apart, we're going into one of the biggest recessions in U.S. history, the unemployment rate is shooting up to ten percent—and you want to start a business to help people find jobs. That's a lot of risk. What helped you take that step, what helped you carry that risk during that time?

Albin: Absolutely. There was a person we met who's first name is Peter, and he would call us naive. He said, "Maybe you're naive enough to succeed," because he didn't think we saw all the factors that you just pointed out. That the recession, in and of itself, to start a non-profit, so we're going to be asking people for money when everybody has much less money, was just a--instead of a for profit company, which you can then charge for a service, was something that I think was very striking to many people along the creation of LAHH. What helped to take that step, or to take on that risk, was, if you go back to that, and maybe you can have an experience similar in your life, but when that question arose in me—What am I doing with my time and talent and experience?—it was a very hopeful question, to keep taking steps because I wanted to find the answer. I wanted to continue to answer that question. It wasn't enough just to say, Well, this is family entertainment, I could watch a movie with my grandma or my niece, I'm not gonna offend anybody, there's going to be some type of moral lesson which I probably won't disagree with, so I'm putting my efforts to good use. I'm in Los Angeles: it's either, like, aerospace or entertainment, so I'm in a good field. I couldn't honestly have stopped at that and said, Yes, this is enough, this is the answer to the question. So the companionship with Guido, our dear friendship, was also something that allowed that risk to be accepted, for the most part with calm and serenity, understanding that it's a journey. That characteristic was extremely apparent to both of us. It's not going to be accomplished overnight: we made the decision early on to keep our jobs at Walt Disney and write the business plan in the evenings and weekends so financially I could support myself and he could support himself. Sure, it took a lot of our free time. But it wasn't something asked of me that I couldn't do. I would say that's a characteristic of my faith. I haven't really been asked something that is totally unreasonable and beyond what I can respond. And even my response may be less than what someone else can give. It was reasonable for me to spend my time this way because it was connected completely to answering that question. We learned dependence, which is beautiful when you really learn it. We asked for help. We asked for help on almost everything. We would go from person to person to person, and would follow the advice that people gave us. I can name all the names. When we finally met Peter, who would give us the office, he said, "Just improve it and you can have it; that's your rent for the first six months." I should have tried to get twelve months, but we took six. [*laughter*] I tried to get six more months and he said, "You're actually asking me to give you more free rein,"and I said, "Yes," and he said, "No." [*laughter*] Fair. I should've asked at the beginning, but it's okay. We got six.

I was comfortable with dependence, I was comfortable with asking, I was comfortable with not having the answer. Guido and I both studied finance and accounting, we didn't study social services. We don't have family members who have disabilities. We didn't spend that much time with people with disabilities, and now we are also employing veterans with disabilities, so there' all of the war-related trauma. In some ways, you could say we were really very, very stupid, or that we were taking an extreme amount of risk. These factors were part of the journey, but I never felt like they were the endgame, like we're gonna end on the fact that we don't have something we need. Instead, I realized that we needed to ask for it. We even went so far as to ask three different people to review our business plan; and secretly among us we had decided we were going to stop if they said, "You guys are totally out of your minds," or "You totally haven't understood the industry." We knew that these were three reasonable people; if they'd told us it wasn't feasible, we'd have kept our jobs.

These three people embraced us, and encouraged us to keep going. It's beautiful to depend. It's beautiful to understand that I'm not alone in front of this big unknown, this big risk. That's a huge gift that I received and I still receive today. We have twenty-eight employees; it's just two of us most of the time in the office. At Disney I had, like—if I could show you an org chart I would—all of my departments and resources mapped out. If I needed something, I knew who to call within the company and get my answer pretty quickly. The org chart of LAHH is pretty simple. [*laughter*] If Guido doesn't know, who am I going to call? Even that made us reach out to other nonprofits and I can tell you that it's one of the most collaborative industries. People gave us their HR paperwork as copies, people let us do interviewing with them to understand the laws and regulations in California, which is, of course, "progressive," we'll just say. We're the most legislated and regulated employment market there is, so we could be easily sued. That realization came quickly: we'll make a mistake and be sued and just shut down. I would say those factors allowed the risk to not seem overwhelming, but instead to really be part of the characteristic of this.

My last day at Disney was August 8, 2008. My first day at LAHH was August 11. I just took off the weekend. Guido went to Rimini and took off like, three weeks. [*laughter*] When I would go in this office, I had to say, "This didn't exist before, now it exists." Walls were painted, he put three windows in, he gave us a different floor. I mean, I had to recognize I didn't do any of the hard labor to make the office exist and here it is, and I have keys. It still is a moment of real awareness of the concreteness of it all. Of course, it doesn't happen overnight, but step by step, and keeping the question open, the desire, is essential, because each step you relate back to becomes an answer, if only partially. The desire grows, so you want to find out more.

I can't deny that everyone goes to work. It's still impressive to me that everyone goes to work, every night, or every day. I thought for sure they'd quit. They're going to say that we don't know what we're doing, and they're going to quit. But they go to work. I don't know. We have enough money for payroll, and that's amazing. Every month we pay the bills. I don't know about you, but I recognize that I didn't make all of this happen by myself. I'm a steward, I need to be in service, I need to have a poverty, a spirit of poverty, for these things. It's an education that, without the risk, I think I would not have the depth of what is this reality in front of me. I think I would take it much more for granted if it had been a lot easier.

Sareen: That's great. Thanks, Nancy. And Andreas, for you as well, this question of risk—we had a chance to talk a couple of times and you have a certain, I think, natural optimism and a certain energy when you start talking about entrepreneurship and your students and your experiences. Still, in all the things you've done, there's clearly some element of risk. I mean, an entrepreneur takes a lot of risk, right? And so, some things have worked out, some things haven't, in your experience as well. How have you lived the problem of risk?

Widmer: I wouldn't call it risk. I mentioned before one of the key aspects that we need to understand, which ails our world and our business community today: Where do people take their self-identity and self-esteem awareness from? If it's from your school and your grades or from, you know—the first thing we ask when we meet is: What do you do? The first thing we ought to ask is: Who are you? I'm a son of God, I'm a child of God. I have dignity because I was made in the image and likeness of God. It's pretty cool, huh? Try to top that. [*laughter*] My quest, and this is sort of what John Paul conveyed—my quest for meaning and for self-esteem rests with that. Now, beyond that, I'm given opportunities. I don't like to call this risk, because that same God who made me in his image gave me all of my talents, and my physical attributes, and just all the dimensions of who I am. All the way to my hair, in which I was luckier than you [*points at Sareen*] [*laughter*], but not as lucky as her—and to my size, to where I was born, when I was born, to every one of my talents and non-talents—I mean, I could never do what you're doing; I can't count to ten without making a mistake. All of these God gave me when I was born. It's like God gave me a box of crayons when I was born. Then God said—and this is the thing: I know there's a lot of young people here and, you know, the most common prayer God hears is probably, "What do you want me to do? What do you want me to do?" Right? Just tell me what to do and I'll do it. God doesn't do that. God looks at you and says, Well, look, I gave you all these crayons, I want you to draw and color. And you say, Well, what do you want me to draw? Well, I don't care what you draw—just draw. It's like when I give this to my son, what do I want from him? Think of yourself, all these kids out there, we have crayons out there, what do you want them to do? Do you want to paint with one color, or all the colors? All the colors. What God is asking us to do is, he gives us a blank canvas and all these crayons and says, This is your life, paint it. Paint your heart out. This is your opportunity to express yourself. Some colors are dark, some colors are black, and you're asked to paint with those; this is not a risk—this is an opportunity. The challenge, and that's where the circle ends again, it starts with us being made in the image and likeness of God. This is a gift, and it ends with the question of who we you paint for. Do you paint with all of these gifts that God gives you, for yourself? Or for God? Many people are gifted with talents that make a lot of money with investments, or they know how to count money, and teach people how to make this. Or in art and they become immensely successful in everything. That's a celebration of our being made in the image of God. The question is: What do you do with this? John Paul was a gifted man. He had so many crayons and painted, I'm telling you, in broad strokes, and it was beautiful, beautiful. Then, when he had the success and the admiration—like from myself, he was my idol, if you wish—he wouldn't take it. He would point to Christ. So, with all your crayons, all the things you paint are beautiful. It's not a risk, it's an opportunity. The risk is when you receive success, and when you are successful at what you do, and if you paint with all the crayons, you will be. The risk is: Will you then point to Christ, or do you take this for yourself?

That's what I learned from John Paul. Risk is a negative word because it has to do with failure and with criticism. Don't be a critic of yourself, be a coach. You know a coach is tough. But the coach has a conviction that you can do it. You can do it. Your nonprofit is going to be very successful. And now what you need, and what you had in these people who are reviewing your business plan—these were coaches. But they probably did tell you some things that you needed to fix, but they started off with every confidence that you could do it. What ails us today is this vision of humanity as a problem rather than a solution. If I'm honest, I see this in my students at CUA. Often in our approach to ourselves we look at ourselves as a problem rather than a solution. Humanity is the solution.

Sareen: Thank you. Let's move on to the theme of this talk: business. Doing business in uncharted waters. Nancy, maybe you can tell us a little bit more what you do in your business. You're part of a nonprofit organization that works with for-profit businesses. What is that like?

Albin: Well, when you're the non-profit in the room, and you're with for-profits, sometimes you're kind of the—sometimes you can be the charitable work in the room, because you have a social mission. Maybe you're technically not as great as the other guys, or maybe you don't have as many resources as the other guys. What I like very much about LAHH is that Guido had visited a non-profit in Oregon that's been around for many years and has multiple lines of business, over one thousand employees, and they are professional. We modeled after them because we didn't want the organization of LAHH to be something that wouldn't contribute to our employees with disabilities having a technical excellence, a professionalism in their everyday life, a sense of pride, a job well done. We didn't want it to be messy as some non-profits can be, just flying by the seat of our pants. We do two things at LAHH. We provide janitorial services to office buildings and we provide administrative services to a naval hospital in San Diego. For the janitorial side, we're using a system of cleaning that for-profit janitorial companies use, and we attend the same trainings that their executives attend. One of the reasons why we use this system is because one of their philosophies in the janitorial cleaning business is to treat cleaning workers as first-class citizens. When we go to symposium, or a conference, with all of our colleagues or our contemporaries in building services, I'll tell ya what—we win that one. We win in the sense that we treat cleaning workers as first-class citizens. We employ people with disabilities and look at them, simply through our faith, and by doing so we become an authority for the for-profit management teams of these other companies, and affect how they see their own relationships. That's something that was very unexpected. We didn't set out to do that, of course, but when you have this—what you were just saying about the idea of painting in broad strokes and allowing your humanity to be the driving force of your identity and of what you're interested in, even in janitorials, a seemingly unprofessional piece of the for-profit sector.

We strive, as do these other companies, to give room and space for all the employees to really become themselves, with an expression of an identity that is not manufactured or directed by Guido or I, or by the management team. This is an area in which we are looked to as guides. As an example, the United States Postal Service just started using the same cleaning method, and they came to visit us with a union member. Our guys, the developmentally disabled. Maybe the intellectual capacity is not as great as in people with a physical disability; if you ask one of our employees how to get to his house, maybe he can't tell you. But if you ask him to follow, and you train him to follow a job card that tells what time to arrive at this building, he can possibly do it. When we arrived at one of the buildings with the U.S. Postal Service, here comes Mark, one of our guys, around the corner, and without saying anything he looks at Guido, he looks at his watch, and he says, "Guido, I'm one minute early." [*laughter*] Let me tell you, you can't deny that. This is a guy with developmental disabilities, pushing a restroom cart, he's one minute early; then he talked to us for one minute and said, "I gotta go"—right in the middle of some question! [*laughter*] I mean, that's something we celebrate; that would be a success for us. That's something that you can't necessarily relate to the bottom line, or you can't relate it to donations or contributions, or you couldn't relate it to when we invoice for that service, what's the percentage of overhead, etc. But that, in and of itself, is the expression of the humanity of that man, in these broad strokes. What we've done is try to set him up to have this experience of achievement. An experience of being confident in what he's doing. For-profits like GMI, or school districts, a lot of universities use this. The reason for them to use this was to save money on the bottom line, it's just a better system and is much more efficient. But for us, our success would be that Mark arrived one minute early, he talked to us for one minute, and then he continued, with a joy and with a smile. It wasn't a heaviness, he was very proud of himself, as he should have been. That's been a very unexpected and wonderful relationship that's developed with our for-profit contemporaries, which we never could have expected. And it's to be shared, too. You let people come and meet you. You let people be a part of that, because everyone goes away and they're silent: we're not in front of a painting, or the Dolomites, we're in front of a guy with a restroom cart who's on time and who's extremely happy about that.

Sareen: Andreas, when I first read this title, "Doing Business in Uncharted Waters," and heard your story—you kind of fit this really well. You've been all over the world doing business in all kinds of places, and you kind of live, breathe, and teach business. So can you share some of your experiences? And are there any common elements of your time as entrepreneur, philanthropist, and professor that kind of jump out?

Widmer: I think every business is a for-profit business. I would challenge you to create your company into a for-profit company. Because by separating the two, think of what we're doing: this is non-profit, this is for-profit—what's the difference? Does it mean in a for-profit company we can't be nice to a guy like that, who actually is on time and probably a very profitable employee at the end of the day? Do we give a halo to one group, or did we see that some people behaved so badly in the for-profit world that we're going to take our bag and go somewhere else and say, You know what, the good ones are over here? We cede the territory of for-profit companies to those who abuse it and who do bad, who have bad intentions. I'm not ready and I'm not willing to cede that space. I believe that if you're looking at the true, and the really good, long-term successful companies, they are person-centered companies. In our own entrepreneurship program at CUA, I'm teaching how you create person-centered companies. I call that centerpreneurship; putting the person at the center of what you do. Because, think about it: it used to be that land was the most important thing in business, and then it started to be work, the trades and all of that, and with shear physical force. Then, you had capital that ruled the day; today it's knowledge. We're in a knowledge economy. We're in an innovation economy. We're in an economy that depends. Our best raw material is no longer in the ground, it's not in your bank account, it's right here [*points to his temple*]. And it's right here [*points to his heart*]. It's vision, it's getting participation from people. The thing is, you can't force anybody to participate in a company like this to make it successful.

What you have to do—and John Paul talked a bit about this—you can't have people work for you; you have to have people work with you to reach a common goal, or you're never gonna get ahead in that knowledge economy. You have to create person-centered companies on every level. You have to produce goods that are truly good. You have to create services, provide services that truly serve. You have to provide meaningful work. You have to create good profit. If you don't do this, people will not be willing any longer to follow you. All these large companies that would give the for-profit world a bad name, are shrinking and falling away. And what we are called to do is to educate our young rising stars to go into that environment, and to not cede the space and say, When we work, we don't just make more, we become more. Business exists for man, not man for business. Business is a path to holiness. Business is a force for good. If we do this, we imitate God, we participate—this is the beauty of it.

At CUA, I start a company with every business freshman. My whole spiel, the whole trick of it, is to start with them—I teach this course called Business as a Vocation—I start with them and I start building this little Internet company. Everybody does it. And eventually I take a step back and the business is there, and they get all excited about it, and then I talk to them about Genesis. And I tell them, You see what God does? God has a thought, and then he creates it, and maybe there's a version two, three, or four, but then he creates it, he has this idea, he contemplates it, he works on it, and he gives it a certain independence. Eventually he creates man, gives him full independence, and invites him to be a co-creator; why don't you finish this? I'm gonna hold back a little bit—you were made in my likeness.

Right now, then, your little business is out there, maybe somebody is interacting with it right now. You just—you can't make something out of nothing. But that's what you just did. From neurons firing in your head, to now this reality existing out there, you just participated in God's creative power. And it's my favorite part of the class, because their eyes pop out, because if you recognize this, then you understand what work is about. When you recognize this you're not going to say, Oh, I'm not going to worry about profit anymore. Because God certainly did care and does care about profit. There's no plant that doesn't produce fruit and a surplus, in a sense. But what it does is reorders the priorities. These three priorities of work are pursued at the same time, but they are ordered, just like in our own life. The first priority of anything we do with each other has to be creative because we imitate God. And love is giving. Therefore, we have to create.

The second thing is, it has to be supportive. It has to support legitimate customer needs. It has to support the flourishing of the persons, all the persons involved in it. It has to support. Work is a path to holiness, a path to heaven. Our work and our companies have to support that.

Finally, it has to be rewarding. Physically rewarding. That includes fair wages, fair prices, and fair profit. You can call it good wages, good prices, and good profit. I think we shouldn't split categories on this; there's one category and it's called work. We should all do this together and not give anybody a pass. By us doing something else, we give somebody else a pass to get away by not pursuing what business and work are really about.

Sareen: Great. Thank you. Last question. Again, the theme is about uncharted waters, which says something to me about discovery. In your experience, Nancy, what have you discovered, what's been unexpected in the things that you've seen?

Albins: I would say the depth of the need that we perceive in our employees and, of course, in myself and in Guido, has been a wake-up call or a recognition that—I may be able to articulate what I need when it's lunchtime and I'd like to eat, but the depth of that is a discovery that continues. I feel privileged to be able to share that need with Guido, with our employees, and to share my need also with them. I love it that we do not fix the problems of our employees. Be it the relationship with their family, their relationship with money, the relationship with themselves. We provide a job that's supportive, absolutely, we help to maintain that job, absolutely, doing a lot of different things—but there's not a power variance. I would say I'm just as needy as our employees with disabilities. And the depth of that has shown me that the friendship and understanding the heart has of your reality is phenomenal. The heart of a person with disabilities can understand. One of my guys, Steve, when he came in the office one day, he understood that I was very stressed out. He looked me straight in the eyes and said, "But Nancy, it's going to be okay." He understood me completely in that moment, and he's developmentally disabled. I'm really in awe at the depth of that which exists in each of our employees, to a point where I would say the heart is not disabled. Maybe the mind, maybe the body, sure, but not the heart.

I have another guy, Omeri, who didn't get along with his supervisor at the beginning. Omeri Osso grew up without his parents and now lives with his aunt. He lives in a gang area of L.A., so he has brothers in prison. It's probably very likely that he could have also joined a gang but he has a disability; he had a lot of different support systems and now he works with us. So his supervisor—this was a couple of years ago—we had our annual bowling party and Omeri was the first one to call Ken, the supervisor, who wasn't there because he was sick. Omeri asked him, Are you coming, are you okay? I didn't teach him that. I didn't say, Call Ken, and I didn't say, Be nice to Ken. Throughout the years, we said, This is the job we're hiring you to do, this is the training, we're going to continue training, the emphasis was all there. We don't reach further into the life and try to then solve the problems of family, relationships, the affective questions that all of my guys have. I mean, that's another interesting discovery: it's not as though people with disabilities don't want to get married and have a family. It's not that they don't want to have a house; they want to have a yard, have pets. So there's a real gift we received in being in relationship with them. I have just a few photos if we have enough time.

[OFFICE PHOTO] This is Brandon, there we are in our office. The guys are learning, they're becoming certified as restroom specialists—actually no, that's vacuum specialist because the bags are blue. They're becoming certified vacuum specialists. People with developmental disabilities often have a really hard time focusing and paying attention. Many of these guys don't drive but they're all on time, and they are all paying attention because they understand this is something good for them. That to me is remarkable.

[OFFICE PHOTO] This is Brandon again. He normally doesn't do vacuuming, but we needed him to do vacuuming this day and the equipment is something that we've always tried to educate them on, there's dignity in using the equipment, and there's the correct way or the incorrect way and there's a safe way and correct way. This kid also didn't grow up with his parents, and was around a lot of gang violence, but the relationship with authority, with Guido, is something that is—I love it that they're all looking at how to put on the vacuum; not banal.

[GROUP PHOTO] Here we are in our office after a training. The smile on the face is a recognition, and the arm of Brandon on Steve's shoulder is a recognition that these people love me and are with me. Justin, on the far left, after a training said, I'm very loved here. Again, that discovery of what the heart is and what it can recognize.

[PHOTO OF ANDRE] Andre loves drawing. I get a lot of his drawings. He takes pictures and sends them to me because I'm not on Facebook. But Guido's on Facebook, so a lot of these images are on Guido's Facebook feed, but this kid's passion for drawing is completely related to his job as a janitor, it's not something outside of it. To welcome that in is to welcome in who is Andre.

[PHOTO OF THREE EMPLOYEES] These are three new guys who were hired recently: Ivan, Anthony, and Kean. They're being hired to do janitorial work that's very hard manual labor. They look very, very happy. Again, the heart has understood something.

[PHOTO OF ANTHONY] Here's Anthony in action. He also had a water bottle, which you can't see in the photo, and I was praising him for having a water bottle because we've had a drought in California.

[GROUP PHOTO] The woman in the middle is from Ohio State University. She wanted to come and see how we clean this building, or these three buildings. It's very humbling to have somebody who's in charge of a university take notes on what we're doing.

[PHOTO OF CREW] Here's the same building, a different crew. This is before work. I just love the smiles.

[PHOTO OF CREW] Here's another crew. You'll notice Omeri, that's him in the front. He became Catholic last year. He did everything. He went through two years of RCIA. His aunt invited us. He lives with his aunt and wanted Guido and I to be there. It's moving to us because it's in a neighborhood that's Latino and African-American. You can only imagine in a gigantic Catholic church that was half in Spanish, the Mass, and there's Guido and I standing in front as he's getting baptized. Again, we pray together, absolutely, but we don't evangelize or try to make these people Catholic. Yet, he wanted us to be right up there. It's an amazing experience, the need of the heart, what we can understand of this.

[PHOTO OF THREE PEOPLE] This is a commander of a Coast Guard base that we clean, and she wanted to take a picture with the janitors as she was retiring. Again, I don't think that's normal.

[PHOTO OF TWO MEN WITH CELL PHONES ATTACHED TO THEIR HEADS] Two of our shining stars. Veterans. The guy on the left is a Marine. The guy on the right was in the Navy and controlled planes. Chris and Melvin, they're supposed to be working. They decided to send me this photo to show me how much they're working, because the phone is taped to their face. [*laughter*] But again, it's a recognition that these people around me are for me. One of the problems that veterans face is that they can't find the level of camaraderie that they had within their—I don't know, I was not in the military so you'll have to forgive the lack of terminology—but in your unit, that's the correct word. You don't find that outside. Maybe in the way that Andreas is talking about creating these businesses you could find it. They give their lives for each other in the military, as you all know, and so that's a big problem when coming back into society, because that's not really present in many companies. The profit is the goal, the advancement of the career. For these two guys who had been deployed in Iraq, what you care about are your brothers-in-arms who you want to come home. I had to show you this photo because you would never know that these guys were veterans.

[PHOTO OF GRADUATE] This is Melvin graduating from college. I didn't, of course, help him do his homework, I didn't get him enrolled, we have nothing to do with that. I just hired him for an administrative job down in San Diego. But the fact that it's related to me, shows again what the heart needs, the unexpected depth that you can find in reality. Guido and I are sometimes very poor in front of these guys who have had this experience of war, yet it's something he wanted to share with us.

[GRADUATION PHOTO] He sent me this one, like, a week later. He said, "I forgot to send you the most important one." So I wrote him back: "I'm glad you didn't forget."

[WORK PHOTO] This is Mike, who's one of our supervisors. He's giving help to Brian. It's indicative of him receiving an award.

[AWARDS PHOTO] Outstanding Cleaning Worker Award at a banquet. This is the type of banquet we go to once a year to honor the janitors.

[OFFICE PHOTO] We were helped by our really good friend Jennifer in LA to update our website, as Guido and I know nothing about that. These are the people who had sat in front of us. They are designers, and I said, What do you design? I didn't understand. They're computer scientists. They sat in front of us, and were asking us questions in such a way that I understood their desire for design was enough, and so we could give 'em our website, our brand, our image, and they could put it together. We spent an hour with them, and the passion that they have for their own work is that indication that our humanity is not a problem but a solution.

[OFFICE PHOTO] And I just really like their office and their exposed concrete.

[BEACH GROUP PHOTO] Lastly, we went to the beach with these guys because we wanted to have a moment of introducing them to beauty. I was being closed one day, and couldn't think of what to do, and then I remembered: We have the Pacific Ocean. [*laughter*] Got it! And it's close. It's a ten-minute drive, so in moments I've been closed I've been helped greatly. We asked Father Jose to come out to help us be introduced to what happens to you in front of something beautiful. These are guys with developmental disabilities, and it's just amazing to see how the heart is constantly in a search. The heart is constantly trying to discover. And this, through work, is something that I never expected: the beauty of the humanity is so tangible, right there in front of me in a way that I never expected.

Sareen: Wow. That's really amazing. [*applause*] I think we're running a little tight here on time, but maybe you could offer just a few thoughts also to that last question about discovery.

Widmer: We make a big mistake, sometimes, by trying to help with fighting poverty or help people with disabilities, and sometimes helping hurts. You said in some of our conversations they don't want to be your charity *du jour*, right? It's very demeaning. We take dignity away from people when we do this, when they become our project. We do this a lot to poor people, be it all the way over in Africa, or in Asia, South America, or right here. It leaves an impression, especially when we try to say, Well, we're gonna do economic development or help or something; it leaves an impression of—if you look at some of our programs and some of our even well-intentioned ways of trying to help, it leaves always the impression in me that we think that they're dumb. We think poor people are stupid. Look around, we think they are helpless, they can't help themselves and they're missing something. One of the most enlightening things that John Paul said on this topic was, if I look around at poverty, it's not a matter of dollars. If you measure somebody's life in dollars and cents, like this person lives on one dollar a day, this person lives on two dollars a day, it's the wrong problem statement. If you make that statement, you're logically calling for a redistribution of wealth. Which is actually a fallacy because our economy is a wealth factory. The more we do business with each other, the more money there is. The money is not a fixed pie; we're a pie factory, we make money. We call it making money. We need to do business with each other. We need to work with each other. That's how you get out of poverty. John Paul said, Don't do this measurement of dollars-a-day-per-person, because it's demeaning, undignified, and, by the way, it's begging the wrong solution. They asked him, "How would you define poverty?" And John Paul said, To be poor is to be excluded from networks of productivity and exchange. To be poor is to be excluded from networks of productivity and exchange. You know what Nancy does for these people? She's including, she's providing them, she's integrating them into a network of productivity and exchange. And it's not somebody else's network. It's normal companies. She's competing like everybody else in a normal market because these people have what it takes to compete. They have a value proposition for the normal market. What we usually do is destructive: we keep the poor over there, and as long as we say we give them a little bit of charity, then we can leave them there. The true solidarity that the Church calls us to requires us to go there and bring them into our networks of productivity and exchange. Include them in our investment plans, include them in our company. Include them in our church, include them in our home. That's a solution to poverty.

Sareen: Well great, thank you, both of you, for your comments. Just a couple of final thoughts. When I listen to both Nancy and Andreas, there are a couple of things that really stuck out.

One of them, which was provoked initially by Nancy, but then as Andreas talked about his life it emerged there as well, is that the separation that sometimes we think exists between work and charity is really false. Pope Benedict talked about this in his encyclical after the financial crisis and he said, Look: charity doesn't happen after work. It doesn't happen in our spare time, or merely with our spare money. It happens throughout work. Nancy lives this very vividly. What I was struck by is that not only is it in the output, that she's helping these folks who are disenfranchised to find work, but it's also the way in which she looks at them, the charity in which she looks at them. That gaze is the way in which work can be, I think, rediscovered, and renewed in the way that Pope Benedict was suggesting. Andreas lives this in a very dramatic way, I find, in the course of his life. Pope John Paul meets him in a way that changes his life and that catalyzes him to pursue business in a completely different way. Then he writes something about faith out of that experience, and then someone comes to him and says, Listen, I'd like you to run this philanthropy for me; and then those experiences catalyzed him to teach to others those same gifts that he's received. So, this dynamic of work and charity aren't separate from the business of business.

The second thing that kind of jumped out is this idea of risk. They both talked about it differently. But what's apparent is, in Nancy's case it's a friendship with Guido and others. In Andreas's case friendship with Pope John Paul and others. But the commonality is: you are not alone. You don't carry this risk alone in the world of business and in the world of life.

Lastly, the element of discovery. You start with an idea, you're given those crayons, you start to build, you start to try different things, and yet business then reveals something to you that's new, that you didn't expect, that helps you discover something more about yourself as well.

Again, thank you both very much.

NEW YORK
ENCOUNTER

LA PORTE
CAMERON
STANCIL

CAMERON
STANCIL

Crossing to the Other Shore

Stories of desire, sorrow, and forgiveness at the beginning of the Year of Mercy with ***Priscilla La Porte****, sister of Cadet Matthew La Porte, recipient of the Airman Medal for his heroic actions during the April 16, 2007 Virginia Tech shooting;* ***Joshua Stancil****, former inmate; and* ***Fr. Peter John Cameron****, OP. (moderator), Editor-in-Chief of* Magnificat

Introduction

"We need constantly to contemplate the mystery of mercy. It is a wellspring of joy, serenity, and peace. Our salvation depends on it. Mercy: the word reveals the very mystery of the Most Holy Trinity. Mercy: the ultimate and supreme act by which God comes to meet us. Mercy: the fundamental law that dwells in the heart of every person who looks sincerely into the eyes of his brothers and sisters on the path of life. Mercy: the bridge that connects God and man, opening our hearts to a hope of being loved forever despite our sinfulness."
(Pope Francis, *Misericordiae Vultus*, Bull of Indiction of the Extraordinary Jubilee of Mercy)

"This is the ultimate embrace of the Mystery, against which man–even the most distant, the most perverse or the most obscured, the most in the dark–cannot oppose anything, can make no objection. He can abandon it, but in so doing he abandons himself and his own good. The Mystery as mercy remains the last word even on all the awful possibilities of history. For this reason existence expresses itself, as ultimate ideal, in begging. The real protagonist of history is the beggar: Christ who begs for man's heart, and man's heart that begs for Christ."
(Msgr. Luigi Giussani, *Testimony during the meeting of the Pope John Paul II with the ecclesial movements*, May 30, 1998)

Saturday, January 17, 2015

Cameron: Hello, everyone. My name is Father Peter John Cameron, I'm a Dominican priest. I'm very honored to have this wonderful opportunity to present to you two extremely exceptional human beings who are my friends.

Priscilla La Porte is a guidance counselor at a high school committed to educating and transforming students into young women of competence, compassion, and commitment in a Catholic, Felician, Franciscan tradition of leadership and service. She received a B.S. in Human Development and Family Studies from the University of Delaware, and an M.A. in Counseling from Montclair State University.

I want to tell you about the day I met Priscilla. A dear friend of mine is Justin Fatica, who is an exceptional young man heading up a ministry to young people throughout the country called Hard as Nails. He was having a day-long retreat and he asked me if I would go and give a couple of talks at the retreat. So I said, Sure. We're there, we're sitting at the table, and across from me at the table is this beautiful, very quiet young woman. I had no idea who she was. When Justin said that we were now going to have a witness, and that the witness was going to be delivered by Priscilla, I realized that it was this young woman who was going to speak, and I wondered what she was going to say. Then, I nearly fell off my chair. Priscilla told us she was the sister of Air Force Cadet Matthew Joseph La Porte, the twenty-year-old Air Force cadet who was murdered on April 16, 2007, in the Virginia Tech shooting that claimed the lives of thirty-two students. I was particularly struck, because almost immediately in her talk Priscilla began to make reference to the Sandy Hook school shooting, which had happened just six months before. That was the place, St. Rose of Lima, where I had been helping out on Sundays, so this was a bit of an open wound for me and I was amazed that Priscilla would have them in mind as she began to talk to us about her own experience.

Then this astonishing young woman also spoke about her mother, Barbara, who is here with her husband, Joe, and that meditating on how God is merciful was one of the only things that helped her family get through their suffering. I wrote down one of the things—well, I wrote down a lot of the things that Priscilla said, but I wanted to tell you this one because

I want her to tell you the rest. She said this, with an exquisite simplicity and authority. She said, "I know real pain." And then she said, "I hope that everyone can see God as merciful. He really is there to carry you through, He's there for you."

Joshua Stancil, after serving an eighteen-year sentence, is currently a candidate for a B.A. degree in English at Arizona State University. Last night he was taking his Italian exam. His writings have appeared in *Magnificat*, and the monthly magazine of Communion and Liberation, *Traces*. Both Joshua and Priscilla have written pieces for the *Magnificat Year of Mercy Companion*.

I first met Joshua in November of 2007, when I visited him at a prison in North Carolina. A friend of mine in the movement Communion and Liberation, who lives in North Carolina, his name is Rob Jones, helped me to arrange the visit. In an email he sent to me in August of 2007, Rob wrote, "I assure you that after you meet Joshua you won't be able to stay away from him." [*laughter*] He said, "He is like a magnet." Rob volunteered to drive me from the airport to the prison and back again. As we're pulling onto the prison property, Rob gave me some excellent advice. He said, Listen carefully to everything that Joshua says, pay attention to everything. Try to remember it all, and when you come out, as soon as you can after your visit, write it all down. I could tell from the seriousness in his voice that this was something that I really needed to do, so I did. And here is the paper [*holds up a paper with notes*]. Immediately after this event it goes right back in the vault. [*laughter*] This is what I wrote down. That the sergeant who admitted me into the visiting room had blonde hair, and said that Joshua was a good inmate. The room was big, with yellow cinderblock walls. There were yellow and green plastic chairs stacked around the room. The temperature in the room was about eighty degrees. Joshua's first words were words of thankfulness. He told me that he had learned to overcome skepticism by thinking about Josephine Bakhita, the Sudanese-born saint who had been abducted as a youth, sold into slavery, tortured, and then finally was ransomed by Christian people who helped change her life and enabled her to find her vocation as a religious sister. He told me that he loved Carthusian monks. He told me that the prison guards would regularly open the inmates' mail and read it before passing it on to the inmates. And he told me that the prison guards thought that the movement of Communion and Liberation was a political terrorist plot. [*laughter*] He asked me to contact his mother, which I did, and Rob Jones was right. Joshua Stancil is like a magnet, and now you can find out for yourself. [*applause*]

Stancil: Prepare to be underwhelmed. [*laughter*] I had no idea he wrote all that down. I can't believe I'm here. I'm sharing a hotel room with a friend of mine named Brian, who was in prison with me. Last night we received a visit from a friend of ours, Michele, who stopped by to say hi, and after she left, Brian and I just sat on our beds looking at each other for a minute, and finally we just said, How strange is our life, and how beautiful. We shared a cell block, and now we're sharing a hotel at the New York Encounter. How did we get to the New York Encounter? I had the same sensation a month ago. I was in Italy: through a bizarre series of coincidences I was able to attend Mass with Pope Francis at St. Peter's Basilica, the only time during the month there that I really got overwhelmed with emotion. Otherwise, I was overwhelmed with exhaustion for most of the trip. But I thought, How did I get here? What series of steps did it take for me to get here? I thought about it last night when Brian and I were in the room talking, how strange and how beautiful life is.

Well, this is basically how I got here. In 1996 I was arrested and eventually sentenced to eighteen-to-twenty-two years in prison. When you're sentenced to prison, particularly if it's for a long time, you cope the best way you can. And for me, the way I did it was simply to go into denial. The law I had broken was a new statute. It had only been on the books for nine months when I was arrested. I'd read some newspaper articles about the law, and it had been somewhat controversial because of the severity of the punishment imposed. So I convinced myself, against any and all evidence, that the legislature was going to revisit this law, revise this law, my sentence would be revised, and I would go home. I just wasn't going to do eighteen years in prison.

After about six years, reality came crashing down: in fact I *was* going to do eighteen years. Compounding the problem was the fact that North Carolina moves you around from prison to prison every three or four years, because they're worried about relationships developing between inmates and staff. They don't want a guard bringing an inmate a cellphone or drugs, and there's the potential for romantic relationships. So I got sent to this really heinous prison. It was very violent and chaotic, and although I was very fortunate and nothing ever happened to me, it was just a...living in that environment day in, day out, and realizing finally that I was going to be in prison for at least another twelve years—I just became despondent.

The only thing that had kept me afloat were some writings of Father Giussani that I had found in *Magnificat*. Just a brief story about how I acquired my first *Magnificat*. It was December of 2000. They sent out some free sample issues, two-week sample issues, and I was very captivated by it but couldn't afford it. I made a dollar a day. So I wrote him a letter and explained the situation: I'm an inmate, and can I order these on a monthly basis? A per issue basis? He wrote back, said, "Don't worry about it, I'll send it to you free for a year." He wound up sending it to me free for about six years. [*laughter*]

Cameron: [*to the audience*] Don't get any ideas. [*laughter*]

Stancil: I quickly gravitated to it. If you're not familiar with *Magnificat*, it's really indispensable—free plug. They have a meditation for each day written by a saint or prominent person in the Church. I quickly gravitated to these little excerpts from the writings of Father Luigi Giussani. I had no idea who this man was. Little bio at the bottom of the page said he was a priest in Milan, and that he was the founder of the ecclesial movement, Communion and Liberation. Well, I didn't care about Communion and Liberation, because I believed myself very macho at the time and independent, and I didn't need friends. Also, my idea of freedom at the time was an absence of ties, complete detachment from anyone and anything. I didn't care about CL, but I was really curious about *him*, and I wanted to know if he had any books in English. I began writing different prison ministries and different Catholic organizations, asking, Do you know who this guy is, does he have any books in English, and how can I order them? Well, when you're in prison and you write letters to people in organizations, frequently they don't write back, because they think you're out for money, or you're trying to work some sort of scam. Most of the people just didn't respond. I heard from a couple of organizations who said, We don't know who he is, sorry, can't help you. I kind of forgot about it.

By the summer of 2002 I'd been locked up about six years, and I was at a horrible prison. Reality, like I said, came crashing down and I became, frankly, suicidal. North Carolina has three different custody levels in its prisons. Close custody, Medium, and Minimum. When you're in Close Custody, you have your own cell, everything's very restricted, there's no privacy. Committing suicide is a relatively easy thing in Close Custody, because you have your own cell, things are more secluded, guards only make one circuit around the block every hour. But I was in Medium Custody, at a prison where the room was open like this one, and you've got fifty bunks in there and the showers are open, the bathrooms are open, just everything is open. I didn't really know what to do. I was going through my locker one day and I found this four-week preparation to make an act of consecration to the Virgin Mary. It had been written by Saint Maximilian Kolbe, who had been my confirmation saint. It was now a month away from the Feast of the Assumption and I thought, Okay, I'll do this. So I did. On the Feast of the Assumption in 2002 I made this act of consecration, and I felt nothing. There was no sense of catharsis or relief. There was no emotion, no joy, no happiness. It was just a complete act of desperation. I was numb.

About two weeks later, I get this letter in the mail from a prison ministry that was responding to an earlier letter of mine about Father Giussani. They said, We don't know who this guy is, or anything about his movement, but we found three email addresses for you, three contact email addresses. I saw the names of three people: John McCarthy, Barry Stohlman, and Rick Kushner. Although I was happy about this on the one hand, on the other hand, if you're in prison in North Carolina you don't have access to the Internet. I thought, Well, a fat lot of good this does me. But then I thought, Okay, here's what I'll do: I'll just pick a name, I'll write a letter, send it to my mom, she can email it. So I just sort of eeny, meeny, miny mo'ed it and I settled on Rick Kushner. I thought, Well, that's a nice Jewish name. [*laughter*] It really was a completely random thing. I wrote this little letter, sent it to my mom and quickly forgot about it. Because I love my mom, but...you know, asking her to do something like this is like rolling the dice. It may happen, it may not. She could be very enthusiastic about doing something, and all yes, yes, yes—and then forget about it. So I forgot about it.

I found out much later that she did send the email. She's not Catholic, so the date would not have been significant for her, but she emailed it on October 7, 2002. October 7 is a feast of Mary, a feast of the rosary. Anyway, I don't know that she has sent this email. Rick receives the email, he contacts a woman named Elisabetta who, together with him, puts together this big box of stuff for me. Some books by Father Giussani, some issues of *Traces*, which is the magazine of Communion and Liberation. Unfortunately, they also included some music CDs, which the prison system in North Carolina does not allow. If you're an inmate you can't have music CDs. So the prison rejected this box, and I don't know anything about it. I don't know my mother has sent the email, I don't know that Rick has got it, I don't know they put the box together, I don't know the prison has rejected it—I'm completely in the dark. Then I get this letter from a guy in Italy name Giorgio Vittadini. It's not every day an inmate in a podunk prison in North Carolina gets a letter from a guy in Italy. I have no idea why he's writing me and I don't really want to write back. One, I don't know what to say. And two, again, I was very macho, independent, I don't want any contact. Unfortunately, I'm from the South, and we're just very polite. [*laughter*] And so I thought, I have to respond, but I don't know what to write about. That night I watched the CBS Evening News and saw that Mount Etna was erupting in Italy. I thought, Well, there's something. [*laughter*] And demonstrating a deep, profound, and embarrassing ignorance of Italian geography, I told Giorgio to *please* be careful about the eruption of Mount Etna. [*laughter*] Like the man's house is built on the lip of the volcano.

A couple of weeks later, now it's November of 2002, and unexpectedly I'm transferred again, but to a much, much better prison. I mean, it's still prison, but it's a much, much better prison. I get this letter from Elisabetta, she explains the whole thing that happened with the box and the rejection of it, and then she says, Hey, would you mind if me and a friend come down to visit you? And again, my instinct is to say, well, No, I just want a book—I don't want problems, it doesn't have to be free, I'll just pay you for it. Basically, I'm here today at the New York Encounter because I just wanted a book. [*laughter*] That's really what this is about. I wanted to say

No, I don't want a visit, but I'm from the South, and we have to be very polite, so I said Yes.

On December 29, 2002, Elisabetta Seratoni and Tobias Hoffmann—he's here today, I just saw him before I came out—came down to visit me. Now keep in mind, they're in Maryland and I'm in North Carolina. It's a one way drive of about seven hours or so for them to visit me. I have no idea why they want to come visit. I'm just assuming they're some pious Catholics on a feel-good tour of Southern prisons and they're doing corporal works of mercy [*laughter*] and storing up crowns in heaven or something. We had a really beautiful visit, I thought. I will never forget that date because on that date my life began to change. I didn't know it at the time, and it didn't change overnight, but when they left I thought, That was great, but I'll never see them again. Five weeks later, Theresa and Mary Ellen came to visit, a month after that, Rick Kushner finally came down to visit, and then a month after that, Rob Jones, who [Fr. Cameron] was talking about, and just every month it was someone new. It got to the point that so many people were visiting, I was receiving a visitor every weekend. And after four or five months of this I became very resistant. I didn't tell anyone, but I became very resistant to it for a couple of reasons.

One, there's the whole guilt issue. I'm in prison, and like Peter said to Jesus, "Lord, get away from me, I'm a sinful man." There was that element. And there was also the element of, I'd kind of been raised to believe good things don't last, so why entangle yourself with people if it's not going to last? I thought, I'm getting a visit every weekend from people who are traveling hundreds of miles to visit me, I have at least eleven years left, they're not going to continue to do this. This is going to end at some point, why not just cut the cord now? We'll all be much better off in the long run. But I didn't, because I could recognize there was something in me that was changing, that was different. This was something I really needed. Even if I wanted to live with the illusion of being macho and independent and whatnot, there was something about me that really needed this. The theme of this year's New York Encounter, "Longing for the Sea and Yet Not Afraid"—although in the poem it says "Longing for the Sea and Yet Afraid"—that was me at the time. I was longing for the sea, but I was very afraid that the journey to it wouldn't last. I didn't say anything, though.

After about a year, Rick Kushner and his wife Chiara came down to visit, and she was pregnant. Very pregnant. She was due to give birth in maybe a couple of weeks. They shocked me by asking me to be their child's godfather. I was stunned. I looked at them and said, "Um...you're *aware* I'm in prison, right? [*laughter*] This is not the way to win friends and influence people, you know. People are gonna think you're crazy." But they said it was what they wanted to do, so they did. Gabriella was born a few weeks later, and my parents attended her baptism because I could not. Rick and Chiara brought her to me four or five months later, and she's this little bundle of golden goodness and I get to hold her there in the prison visitation room. She continued to visit me during the rest of my sentence.

I received another letter from Italy, but this one was not from Giorgio Vittadini, it was from Father Giussani himself. It was very brief, a couple of lines long. It was less than two years before his death, he was in very, very bad health. I was deeply moved by this letter even though it was very brief. At one point in the letter he made reference to our faith: *la nostra fede*, and he had underlined the word *nostra*—"our." And I realized that he was associating himself with me in some way, which is an unusual sensation for an inmate to have, because most people don't want to associate themselves with you, which is understandable, I suppose. But I thought, He and I are extremely different: he's Italian, I'm American; he's elderly, I'm young; he's not in prison, I'm in prison; we're separated by thousands of miles. But we share this one experience.

I remember one of the first things I read by him was about verifying the Church's claims for itself. He was going over different ways to verify the Church's claims, and one of the ways that's used by certain religious groups is this idea of an inner enlightenment, that you have this overwhelming sensation, this feeling of forgiveness. And the problem with this is: How do you know it's not just a trick of the mind? If your certainty, your faith, is based on a feeling, what happens when that feeling goes away? Feelings come and go, they rise and fall like an ocean tide; so how can you be sure? Well, when you're sitting in a prison visitation room, and a married couple asks you to be the godfather of their daughter, then you can be sure. Because now love has become flesh, mercy has taken on human flesh, it's become incarnate. Last night, if you weren't here, if you missed the talk with Greg

Wolfe and Christian Wiman—Christian Wiman was talking about how for many, many years he would talk about God sort of abstractedly: "God." But at a certain point he needed something concrete. I realized that was the same thing with me. That it's one thing to read in the Bible that you're forgiven, that mercy exists; it's another thing when you're experiencing it, when mercy comes to you through people with names, such as Elisabetta and Tobias, Theresa and Mary Ellen, Michelle and Sara, Joe and Simonetta and Gabriella and Rose—I could go on and on. Father Peter used to visit me. At that point you know that mercy exists.

On the topic of the mercy—because I think I'm getting long-winded here—when I was in Italy I was talking about the Year of Mercy. I've been aware, looking online, that there are some Catholics for whom Pope Francis is kind of a controversial figure, which is fine, I suppose. Not every Pope can be popular with everyone. But what kind of irks me about some of the criticism is that they even criticize this Jubilee Year of Mercy that he's proclaimed. Their rationale is that Francis talks too much about mercy and not enough about repentance. I thought, You're not really understanding what mercy is. I'm no moral theologian, I'm not an expert, but it seems to me that if the mercy I receive is contingent upon a certain amount of repentance on my part, then in effect I'm earning that mercy—which contradicts the very definition of mercy. Mercy always has to come first.

The example that I used in Italy was the woman caught in adultery. Two thousand years ago, adultery wasn't merely a moral failing, it was a criminal offense and you could be executed for it, if you were a woman. The man got a pass, apparently, but she was going to be executed. She's thrown at the feet of Christ, and one of the most striking things to me about that whole passage is that Jesus never one time calls her an adulterer. He never throws her sin back in her face, he never tries to humiliate her about what she's done. Because she doesn't need to be humiliated; he knows she just needs to be able to start again, and so that's what he lets her do. Mercy always comes first. Romano Guardini once wrote that justice gives structure and order to things, but mercy creates. I think that's one of the points of the Year of Mercy.

A woman came up to me after one of the talks in Italy, and she said, "I don't think Jesus can be merciful to me because I'm like a volcano that just continually erupts. If he's merciful to me today, then I'm gonna waste it because I'm gonna erupt again tomorrow. I'm this volcano that continually erupts." And I said, "So yeah, but volcanoes gave us Hawaii. Out of all that fire and chaos and violence and tumult, came one of the most beautiful places on earth. Christ can use anything." There really are no objections to mercy except our own. Pope Francis provocatively makes reference to Christ's caress of mercy on our sins. And that's been my experience. I realize that the only objection that can be raised is a false one that I come up with. Luckily, I had people who wouldn't let me do that. [*applause*]

Cameron: Priscilla La Porte.

La Porte: Good afternoon. I used to think that being a Christian meant your life was perfect, everything was all together. I thought it was God's way of saying, "Thank you for deciding to follow me." I had a good life. I had a good education. I had friends, I had everything that I needed and was very happy. I had a good relationship with my brother most of the time. He was two years older than me, so sometimes he annoyed me or he picked on me; that's what brothers do. But I looked up to him and I loved him. When I was in high school, he started college at Virginia Tech and I was very proud of him because he had gotten an Air Force scholarship. I knew he was happy, and he was on his way to doing very great things. He was very excited to have a career in the military when he finished.

On April 16, 2007, my senior year, when I woke up it was pouring outside. There was actually so much flooding that school was canceled. We lost power, so I decided to go to my place of work, which was a restaurant, because my boss had a generator. I went in, and there were TV screens there and news was coming in that there was a shooting at Virginia Tech. Initially, it didn't bother me because I knew the school was very big, and this just wasn't something that happened in my life. My life was good. So I didn't even think, Oh my gosh, I wonder if Matt's okay. As the day went on, the news didn't stop and it was getting worse. It wasn't just ten people, it was twenty people, and then it was thirty people, and I was calling my mom, saying, "Did you get in touch with Matt?" And she hadn't. I was trying to call him and he wasn't picking up his phone. It just kind of went on for the rest of the day like that and I kept getting more and more nervous. When I spoke to my mom again, she told me that she spoke to my brother's roommate, and he said that the last time he saw Matt was in the morning when he left for class. He was in the building where the shooting took place and I just collapsed. I didn't know what to do. I couldn't let my mind go there, but it seemed to be going anyway to that place. I left work, and I was yelling at God in the car, saying, "This can't be real, this can't be my life, don't let me find out that something happened to my brother. He has to be in the hospital, maybe he got shot in the foot and that's why we haven't heard from him, or he's helping other people. Because this just can't be real." Later that evening we found out that my brother had died that day. I just remember hearing those words, "I'm so sorry." I really don't remember much after that. I don't know what that night was like, I just don't remember. But months afterwards I remember feeling all that pain. Graduation was coming up because I was a senior, prom was coming up, it was supposed to be a really happy time, but it was just an awful time. My friends' siblings were coming home from college and mine wasn't. It was the loneliest time of my life, because my parents were going through something and I couldn't help them. I couldn't reach out to them. They couldn't help me. We were all broken. My friends were there for me, although they hadn't experienced what I was going through. I didn't know anyone who had experienced what I was experiencing. Matt wasn't around, and I felt like God wasn't around. It was the first time in my life that I just couldn't connect with him, because this wasn't the way that I related to him. I didn't want to be angry with him, I didn't want to shut him out of my life, but it was too painful to approach him because I felt like he let this happen. He said he is good, that he is gonna always be there for me, but how is he there for me? How was he there for my brother?

I started praying the rosary, because there was really nothing left for me to do. I figured Mary kind of went through the same things that I feel like I was going through. I'm sure that Mary was very hurt when she lost her son, and the rosary was structured. I didn't have to think, I could just say it. It was the only time that I felt some little drop of hope, so I kept doing it. I kept praying the rosary, and did it for the future because there was no hope in that moment; but with the rosary I felt like maybe one day I could get there. The pain was just too overwhelming. It felt like I was walking around without any arms or something. It was like I lost this huge part of who I was and I could never get it back. Through the rosary, Mary showed me her heart and what she went through and what Jesus went through, and she said, "It's okay; you can trust Jesus and you can be happy again." She helped me to see Jesus through her eyes and his mercy and his love. I realized that God was carrying this cross with me. He didn't leave me; he was with me the whole time.

It took a while, but I did start talking to God again, and my prayer became, "God, please heal me because I just—I'm so unhappy. I don't want to be a bitter person, I want to be a better person." And God was working through my life for a long time, it hurt for a long time. Some days it still hurts. He was working behind the scenes, though, for many years. I didn't know it then, but on April 9, 2015, my family and I got confirmation that my brother was being awarded that day for his heroism. He had helped to stop the shooter when he entered the classroom. He was being awarded the Airman's Medal from the United States Air Force. There is about a three-minute video that will take you back to that day.

[VIDEO]

That ceremony took place in Blacksburg, Virginia, where my brother is buried. We received the medal on his behalf. It's the highest medal awarded in a non-combat setting, usually involving risk of that person's life, although it does not have to be successful. You can't really tell in the video, but that day was so beautiful; it wasn't just the weather, but just everything was so perfect. There were so many people who came to support Matt and be there for him; many we hadn't even seen for ten years. There were just so many people there it was like a foretaste of heaven. It was one of the happiest days of my life. People were saying, "I'm so sorry," and I was like, "Why are you sorry? I'm so happy." I just remember standing there when everything was being read, and there was a slight breeze, and the sun was shining, and I just felt like God was saying, "How could you think that I would just abandon you? Why would you not trust me?" And I finally felt like God was totally there again, like he was before my brother had passed. That was eight years later. I don't know why it took eight years in the grand scheme of things but God's timing is perfect. I don't think my heart would have been ready to accept it anyway, or I might not have been happy. I don't know. But we have to trust always that God does things the way he does for a reason, and that he'll always make things better. Not just better, he doesn't just restore us, but he gives us a resurrection. We can talk to our friends, we can go to therapy, we can do all these things that can be helpful for us when we're really hurting, but there's nothing like God and what he can do for you when you're in the depths of despair. There's no one that can take something so awful and horrible and have something so beautiful and wonderful come out of it. I just want you to remember that there's always a resurrection, whatever you're facing in life. With God it's gonna be even better than it was before. Of course I miss Matt. Of course I wish he was here, but I have such an appreciation for life now, and I really know what it's about because of everything that's happened in my life. Without Matt and without God, I wouldn't know everything I know now. The legacy that I'm left with and that I try to live by every day is on the back of my brother's prayer card, which I will leave you with.

It's called "The Legacy." I don't know who the author is. [*Editor's note: "The Legacy" is by Merrit Malloy*]

When I die
Give what's left of me away
To children
And old men that wait to die.

And if you need to cry,
Cry for your brother
Walking the street beside you
And when you need me,
Put your arms
Around anyone
And give to them
What you need to give to me.

I want to leave you something,
Something better
Than words

Or sounds.

Look for me
In the people I've known
Or loved,
And if you cannot give me away,
At least let me live in your eyes
And not on your mind.

You can love me most
By letting
Hands touch hands
By letting
Bodies touch bodies
And by letting go
Of children
That need to be free.

Love doesn't die,
People do.
So, when all that's left of me
Is love,
Give me away

Thank you. [*applause*]

Cameron: We have a little bit of time left, so I'd like to ask a question of Priscilla and Joshua. At lunchtime, we had a chance to be together and we were talking about things in preparation for today. I was struck by something sort of odd about the presentation, which is, we have two wildly different sorts of people on either end of the table who are speaking about the same thing. So, we have a person who was incarcerated, he committed a crime. When we think of prisoners we often—they're sort of a symbol for our own tendency to do evil, to commit sins, etc. And that situation is so different from the situation of somebody plunged into a kind of grief that just can't be imagined. That person, if you want to use the word, is a kind of a victim. So there's not sort of an immoral quality to the reason the person is suffering this terrible grief, but the pain can't even be described. And yet, strangely, the antidote for both is the same thing. Joshua had some magnetic things to say about that, so I ask him to talk about it now.

Stancil: We were sitting there having lunch and I was listening to Priscilla's mom talk about her experience, and I was very struck by the fact that she said, "I had to let people be close to me because I realized that's what they needed to do." The same thing had happened to me. So I mentioned to them that I was very struck by the fact that although we're sort of opposite sides of—you know, I had a victim, and they are victims. I didn't know what to do with my guilt and they didn't know what to do with their grief, but the solution was the same for both, which was to allow people, and I would say to allow Christ, to be close to you through people. And that there is some resistance to that, at least there was in me, as I mentioned earlier. Eventually that resistance was overcome. I was just very struck by the fact that it's two very different situations but the solution was the same.

For me, being accompanied even happens when I'm not looking for it, or even when I don't really want it. Like I mentioned, I just came back from Italy, and I knew the return flight to America was going to be packed, and it was. I get to the plane and I'm in seat 43G, which is all the way in the back on the aisle next to the bathroom. [*laughter*] It's a nine-hour flight, and I thought, Well, good luck getting any sleep. But I just want to be alone. Long story short, I get down to my seat, and there's a woman in the middle seat who has her coat over what was to be my seat. I'm assuming she's Italian; most of the people on the flight are. I smile, point to myself, and point to the seat. She smiles, picks her coat up, but she just keeps staring at me. When I finally sit down, she looks at me, and says with this Italian accent, "You're Joshua." [*laughter*] I'm serious.

I don't know what to say. It was surreal. I think, She must have been at one of the talks. And then, as if she's reading my mind, she says, "I wasn't at any of your talks, [*laughter*] but I have a letter from you from a long time ago." And I say, "How do you have a letter from me from a long time ago?"She says, "Well, I'm Lorna." The name doesn't ring a bell, but then she explains a little more and I realize who she is: she used to live in New York City, we exchanged one letter apiece, then she moved back to Italy.

How odd for her to be on the same flight as me, sitting right next to me. But it gets even weirder because she wasn't even supposed to be on that flight. She had been bumped. Her flight was the day before and she got bumped to my flight, into the seat right next to me. I didn't want to be accompanied on that flight, but I realized that it was Jesus telling me he was accompanying me even in that moment. Lorna and I enjoyed a nice flight back. The solution was to be accompanied.

Cameron: I'm very moved by these days here, and I'm especially struck by all the young people who are here. I'm wondering, Priscilla, if you could say something to them, because you're a young person—I don't know if you knew that. [*laughter*] Also, you work with young people. I want to make a little confession before I tell you what I want to tell you. I'm so happy I didn't know your history before I met you, because I would have been terrified. I really wanted to meet Barbara, your mom, and I was really terrified. Because, how do you talk to a person who's not only a mother who's lost a son, but lost a son in such a horrific way? And I'm a believer—I'm a Catholic actually [*laughter*]—so I believe in faith; but I've never been through anything like that. Never been through anything like that. It makes me very scared to come face to face with someone who has suffered that kind of atrocity. And I have to confess to the same sort of terror walking into the prison the first time I went to see Joshua. Not because I was afraid of him, but because of the whole situation. Yet here's the thing: it is people like you, and your mom, and your father, who to me are the greatest authorities on the planet. Because when you speak, you have an absolute viability. It seems to me that only suffering can give that to a person. As we listened to that beautiful Edgar Lee Masters poem, I think young people especially are afflicted by the sense that there is no meaning to life. I do feel alone in my suffering and therefore the thing that I must do is do everything in my power to obliterate suffering from my life—to exterminate it. But it's impossible, obviously. No matter how hard we try, it keeps coming back. Even more important is what Christian Wiman said, that we can't really experience the joy of life without the experience of suffering. In that respect, suffering itself is a kind of mercy. So could you say something to the young people?

La Porte: If nature takes its course, we're going to be here for a number of decades, so we might as well make the most of life. I could've very easily made the choice to just say I'm done and I'm gonna be miserable, because I would have had every reason to do that. Just walk around and be bitter, because there are people like that. Because the only thing that makes them feel better is to know that other people are miserable. I could have done that, but I knew that wasn't the truth. When you're faced with incredible pain, there's no way of getting around the fact that it's horrible and it stinks, and you want to run away from it because it's awful. But you have to hold onto hope that those experiences are what's going to make you a more beautiful person because you've experienced so much. That's also the stuff the world needs to hear about. I don't like telling the story I just told. I do it because I know that it helps people, and that's more important than my comfort. I tell the kids I work with at the high school: You can't give up, you have to share this with people. How many other kids would feel better and more accepted if they knew they weren't the only one? You have to use it to make the world better. What else is going to make the world better? There's so much power behind that. So use it.

Cameron: Are all the young women in your school aware of your story?

La Porte: No, but I do share it when I think it will help them.

Cameron: Can you tell us one story about that? You don't have to reveal names.

La Porte: I don't know if it was anything extraordinary; maybe it was for them, but they're always really shocked—"Oh my gosh." And I think I'm a pretty smiley kinda person, so you would never know what had happened in my life. It's hard for the kids to believe. If they can see me genuinely happy and caring for them, then they know that whatever it is they're going through, they can get to the place that God has helped me get to. [*applause*]

Cameron: Any last thoughts, Joshua? Before we let you take a nap? [*laughter*]

Stancil: One thing that touches on what she said, about allowing suffering to run its course and take it's time. When I was in the county jail waiting to be sentenced, I knew I was looking at around twenty years in prison. My attorney came to me one night and said, "Maybe some good news: the prosecutor doesn't really care about your case that much, and there's a chance your charges will be reduced and you'll just get a sentence of five years or less." So naturally I started praying really hard for the five years or less—but I didn't get that. I got the eighteen to twenty-two years. It would appear, if you don't look at it too closely, that I didn't get what I asked for. It was easy in that moment to feel that I'd been abandoned. But if I'd gotten what I'd prayed for, if I'd gotten that five years, I wouldn't be here now, because I met the Movement in year six. I have a goddaughter because I got the eighteen-year sentence as opposed to the five-year sentence. On the one hand, my suffering might have been less if I'd gotten the five year sentence, but my life would be far less rich, and far, far poorer just in terms of happiness. Suffering is a mystery but it does have a value; in my experience it does.

Cameron: Your suffering would have been less, but our suffering would have been more. We want to thank you, Joshua and Priscilla, very much, for your witnesses and for all you did to help us see the face of Christ. [*applause*]

NEW YORK
ENCOUNTER

SACHS
CHERICO
O'MALLEY

"Setting Out on the Long Path of Renewal" (Pope Francis)

Reflections on Pope Francis's encyclical Laudato Si' (On Care for Our Common Home) *with* ***Sean Cardinal O'Malley****, Archbishop of Boston;* ***Jeffrey Sachs****, Director of the Earth Institute at Columbia University; and* ***Rebecca Vitz Cherico*** *(moderator), Instructor in Spanish Studies, Villanova University*

Introduction

"What kind of world do we want to leave to those who come after us, to children who are now growing up? This question not only concerns the environment in isolation; the issue cannot be approached piecemeal. When we ask ourselves what kind of world we want to leave behind, we think in the first place of its general direction, its meaning and its values. Unless we struggle with these deeper issues, I do not believe that our concern for ecology will produce significant results. We need to see that what is at stake is our own dignity. The issue is one which dramatically affects us."
(Pope Francis, *Laudato Si'*)

Cherico: Good evening, everyone. I'm very happy to welcome you all to this evening's event, which promises to be a fascinating moment of encounter. Before we begin this evening, I'd like to offer a special thank you to Relevant Radio for their collaboration and sponsorship of this event tonight. We also have a special thank you as well to the research cluster in Science and Subjectivity that helped organize the event. And we owe a particular debt of gratitude to a great friend there, Professor Bob Pollack. [*applause*]

Saturday, January 16, 2016

This evening's event, as you know, features a discussion of the Pope's recent encyclical, *Laudato Si'*. *Laudato Si'*, the Pope's second encyclical, was officially published in June of 2015. It takes its title from St. Francis of Assisi's *Canticle of the Sun*. The *Canticle* is both a poem and a prayer, praising God for his creation in all its many manifestations. *Laudato Si'* means "praise be to you" in the dialect Italian of that time. In it, the Pope makes an urgent appeal for shaping the future of our planet.

We are particularly fortunate tonight to have two speakers who are experts on the themes of the encyclical. We will first hear this evening from Dr. Jeffrey Sachs. Professor Sachs is widely considered one of the world's leading experts on economic development and the fight against poverty. He is, among many other titles and honorary degrees—more than twenty—the Director of the Earth Institute, the Quetelet Professor of Sustainable Development, and Professor of Health Policy and Management at Columbia University. He is also Special Advisor to United Nations Secretary-General Ban Ki-moon on the Millennium Development Goals. Professor Sachs is also a frequent contributor to major publications such as the *Financial Times of London*, the *International Herald Tribune*, *Scientific American*, and *Time* magazine. Prior to joining Columbia, Sachs spent over twenty years at Harvard University, most recently as Director of the Center for International Development and the Galen L. Stone Professor of International Trade. A native of Detroit, Michigan, Sachs received his B.A., M.A., and Ph.D. degrees at Harvard.

His Eminence, Seán Cardinal Patrick O'Malley, a Capuchin, was born in 1944 in Lakewood, Ohio, and raised in Western Pennsylvania, where he entered a Franciscan seminary. At twenty-one, he was professed into the Order of Friars Minor Capuchin and at twenty-six he was ordained a Catholic priest. After earning a Master's degree in Religious Education and a Ph.D. in Spanish and

Portuguese Literature from the Catholic University of America, he taught at Catholic University and founded Centro Católico Hispano (Hispanic Catholic Center) in Washington, D.C., an organization that provides educational, medical, and legal help to immigrants.

Since his ordination to the episcopacy on August 2, 1984, he has served as the Bishop of the dioceses of St. Thomas in the Virgin Islands; Fall River, Massachusetts; and Palm Beach, Florida. Pope John Paul II appointed him Archbishop of Boston in July 2003. Pope Benedict XVI named him a Cardinal in 2006.

On April 13, 2013, Pope Francis appointed Cardinal O'Malley to an advisory board of eight Cardinals to help the Pope govern the Catholic Church and reform its central administration.

So, without further ado, as a part-time professor of Spanish at Villanova University, I look forward to learning from both of these men this evening. [*applause*]

Sachs: Thank you very much. An event like this is what's categorized as pure joy. It's a delight to be here, and it's an incredible honor to be here with Cardinal O'Malley. I look forward to our discussion. It's also a joy because *Laudato Si'* is a remarkable encyclical. I think it will be regarded in history as one of the most important encyclicals of modern times. It comes at a moment of profound importance and significance for the world. It's already had an important effect, a very important effect. We're in a difficult situation globally. As everybody knows, the world is not working very well. It's not working very well socially. It's not delivering even the basic needs of more than a billion people on the planet, and at the same time our economic juggernaut is threatening the planet environmentally. Pope Francis already, in his exhortation, his first message, *Evangelii Gaudium*, used a phrase that I think is the most powerful, evocative phrase for our time: he said that what we face today is a globalization of indifference, meaning that with all the profound challenges that we confront, whether it's social exclusion, massive inequalities of income and wealth, or huge numbers of young people who are displaced and dislocated and often can't find any foothold other than ending up in gangs or paramilitaries. With our environmental catastrophe we can't seem to focus on what the Pope is saying. Both the exhortation and this encyclical are remarkably powerful, and are, I think, already successful efforts to break the indifference of people and help them to see what is at stake right now. I say that it's already had a historic effect because Pope Francis issued this encyclical last summer, knowing the world was to immediately confront two major diplomatic challenges. The first, in September of last year, was when the world leaders got together with the intention of adopting a framework of sustainable development. The encyclical helped to ensure that that step would be successful. Not only was the encyclical key, but Pope Francis himself opened the general assembly, as you'll recall, on September 25th, giving a moving and powerful speech to world leaders and then, moments after, the world leaders unanimously endorsed a new framework called the Sustainable Development Goals, which can serve as a framework for global cooperation for the coming generation.

It was just weeks after that, and, of course, in the shadow of the terrorist attack in Paris, when world leaders assembled again in Paris on November 30 to open up two weeks of diplomatic negotiations on climate change. You probably noticed, when walking into the building from our semi-summertime of a New York winter, that something's a little weird. Of course, we are in the midst of the warmest period on Earth in probably—if not thousands of years, then tens of thousands of years. We're deranging the planet, and world leaders have not been able to find a path forward. There are powerful interests and massive confusion about this. Pope Francis has been extremely concerned about that failure, so *Laudato Si'* was also directed towards helping all of the world's leaders understand the gravity of the situation, and the essential morality, the moral obligation, to find a way forward.

As I'm sure you know, last month, on December 12, all one-hundred ninety-six signatories of the U.N. Framework Convention on Climate Change, for the first time ever, agreed on how to implement a climate agreement—what's called the Paris Climate Agreement. I would say, having been part of that process now for several years, that the encyclical played a magnificent role. It did so in a fundamental way, which I just want to explain briefly, and I'll conclude the opening remark with that.

Our greatest problem, expressed by that phrase, "the globalization of indifference," is that we're having a very, very hard time on this planet understanding what's truly important for us. We're living in a period of tremendous technological capacity that makes it possible to do what would seemingly be miraculous things. We really can end extreme poverty on the planet, we can save the lives of millions of children who are dying every year of diseases that are now completely controllable or preventable. And we can transform the world's energy system to a climate-safe energy system by shifting from fossil fuels—coal, oil, and gas—to renewable energy and other low-carbon energy sources.

We have the technological means to do this. As an economist, I can tell you we have the economic means easily to do this. Economists don't know very much except how to count money. I'll tell you the bottom line. Every year, the world economy is producing ten trillion dollars of output. That's a lot, even to a macroeconomist. It's far and away enough to end poverty, fight disease, shift the energy system to safety, and end scourges like human trafficking and modern forms of slavery. These are all within reach. It's our heads that have to get straight on this, not our technological choices, or breaking the bank economically. That is the core message of this encyclical, but it's the core message of the Church's social teachings in modern history.

I wanted to conclude by putting this encyclical into a little bit of historical context. I see this encyclical as the latest on a path that started in 1891 with *Rerum Novarum*, which was the first social teaching of the Church on "new things." And the new things of *Rerum Novarum* were the new things of the industrial revolution. The Church made a central assertion back in 1891 which it has carried forward consistently for a hundred and twenty-five years. It's a crucial assertion in my view. It is that an economy can only function if it functions within a moral framework. A market economy just left to profit-seeking will never deliver human benefit by itself. It will run wild. It will empower the too-powerful. It will leave the poor to die. It will destroy the natural environment. Unlike what a bad Economics 101 textbook would teach about the invisible hand and the market economy, the economy cannot take care of itself except if it's within a moral framework. The Church has put forward powerful standards starting with the preferential option for the poor, and with the doctrine of the universal destination of goods, which in essence for an economist means that private property is for human purpose; it's not sacrosanct, if I may say so. It is a method of institutions, but, it doesn't serve as an end in itself. Morality has to be the primary standard for how an economy functions. From *Rerum Novarum* onward there have been several profound teachings about how an economy can fit within a moral framework, and how statecraft can fit within a moral framework. I would point to Pope John XXIII's 1963 encyclical, *Pacem in Terris*, which said that state-to-state relations are not just a game of politics or diplomacy, they also have to operate within a moral framework.

I had the great honor to be on an advisory team in 1991, in helping to prepare preliminary documents for *Centesimus Annus*, which was the hundredth anniversary of *Rerum Novarum*, and came at the moment of the end of the communist domination of Eastern Europe. Where Pope John Paul II was called upon to give guidance was to insist that a market economy be seen the right way, and only within a moral framework: not just a market by itself, but a market economy guided by morality. I see *Laudato Si'* in that profound tradition. What Pope Francis is saying here is that the market economy also must live within the boundaries of the physical creation. We cannot destroy the climate, the biodiversity, the earth's ecosystems, and say that's just property rights, that's just a market economy. The economy has to be bound by the fundamental morality of protecting the creation and protecting the planet and furthering human well-being.

The encyclical is brilliant in reading, in text, in analysis. I could assign Chapter One of this encyclical just in the introductory science class, because it is fully, thoroughly, science-based on what's happening to the ecosystems, on how to understand climate change, and on how to understand the loss of biodiversity. But then it takes that scientific base and, of course, puts it in the moral framework and calls on us, in the two concluding chapters, to find what Pope Francis calls a common plan for our common home. In the final chapter it calls on us to educate each other and young people to understand what it means to live with integral development or sustainable development.

As a professor of sustainable development, you can't ask for more than that kind of call. The world is heeding Pope Francis' call, because we are step-by-step finding a way to find that common plan. I have to say, and I have to explain as a U.N. official, that in these conferences there are a hundred and ninety-three member states of the U.N. There are actually a hundred and ninety-three signatories to the climate convention. If any one country stands up and objects, under the rather odd rules of the game, that can stymie everything. So when you reach an agreement, as was reached in Paris on December 12—I don't know if I'm speaking technically, but I'll say it was a small miracle. [*laughter*] And it was a miracle that had inspiration from *Laudato Si'*. That's why we're here tonight enjoying this wonderful document. [*applause*]

Cherico: Thank you very much. Now I turn the mic over to Cardinal O'Malley.

O'Malley: Thank you very much, Rebecca. Thank you, Professor Sachs. We want to say thank you to the organizers, El Quentro, for bringing us here to reflect on this very important topic. I often share with people the story of a Jesuit and a Franciscan who are walking down the street one day and confronted by a young man who says, "Fathers, what novena do I have to make to get a BMW?" [*laughter*] The Franciscan says, "What's a BMW?" And the Jesuit says, "What's a novena?" [*laughter*]

Well, we are very blessed with a Pope who is a Jesuit through and through and represents the treasures of Ignatian spirituality, but at the same time is very Franciscan. The choice of his name as Francis, when he became our Holy Father, was a clear signal of what his pontificate was going to be about. We see in Francis a man who had such an awareness of the fatherhood of God, and that is sort of the central theme in the spirituality of St. Francis, which allowed him to realize that his call was to be a universal brother, and to work for peace among all people. To have a very special love for the poor and a love for creation. It's therefore not surprising that the encyclical has been named *Laudato Si'*, but it's very unusual. Encyclicals usually have these Latin names from the first phrase in the encyclical. But the Holy Father has chosen the first words of the *Canticle of Brother Sun*, which, by the way, is probably the first piece of Italian literature in history, because prior to that, everything was written in Latin. It's certainly the oldest Italian writing that we have. The Holy Father is quoting from this beautiful canticle, as Rebecca pointed out.

St. Francis actually wrote when he was very sick, he was in a little hut that St. Clare and the sisters had built for him at San Damiano. He was already blind. St. Francis died very young and he lost his sight long before he died. So this is a man talking about the beauties of creation, but seeing that beauty in his heart because with his eyes he could no longer see it. When he died in 1226, he wanted to die lying naked on the ground at the Portiuncula, and asked the friars to sing this song to him. They added a phrase after, calling upon Brother Sun, Brother Moon, Sister Water, and Brother Fire, and they added a verse about Sister Death, because Francis saw death as not something terrible, but someone who ushers us into God's presence.

And so the Holy Father has chosen the name that is a hymn of communion of creation. I'm sure that when the Holy Father first announced this encyclical, all of us thought this was going to be a great gift to the Church and it will make us feel very proud to be Catholics. But in the months since the encyclical has been released, I've come to see that *Laudato Si'* is a gift not just to the Church, but to the whole world. And the broader source of the significance of the encyclical has come in part from the way that the secular media, the academic and scientific communities, and the public in general have received the words of Pope Francis. A typically striking example of this reception was a quote from *The Guardian* newspaper in London, which called the encyclical, "the most astonishing and perhaps the most ambitious papal document of the past one-hundred years." One of the secular publishers that released the document invited Professor Naomi Oreskes, a professor of History of Science at Harvard, to write an introduction, and she begins it by saying, "Sometimes, however, a book catalyzes thought into action. *Uncle*

Tom's Cabin did this and so did *Silent Spring*. Like these works, Pope Francis' encyclical is a call to action that insists that we embrace the moral dimensions of problems that have heretofore been viewed primarily as scientific, technological, and economic."

My intention tonight is not to provide a comprehensive assessment of this compelling teaching document; but rather I wish to lift up some pieces of the encyclical, encouraging you to pursue their meaning in greater depth. Specifically, I will comment on how this encyclical fits into the longer tradition of Catholic social teaching that the professor has already mentioned. Then I will highlight the distinctive moral analysis, which Francis provides for addressing the challenge of environment. And finally I will focus on the particular religious resources that the Holy Father offers all of us—Catholics, Christians, religious traditions, and others drawn to this vital issue but not related in our religious convictions. Pope Francis locates his reflection on the environmental crisis solidly in the lives of his immediate predecessors on the Chair of Peter. Citing St. Paul, John Paul II, and Pope Benedict, often he illustrates that this encyclical is not the first time that the Church has addressed the environment. To be sure, he's correct. But it's also useful to point out that in the one hundred twenty-five years of social teaching, reaching from Leo XIII through Pope Benedict, the issue of environmental challenge as a religious moral question has not received the kind of attention that issues of social justice, human rights, war and peace have received from the Magisterium. Indeed, Pope Francis uses an interesting analogy which I will expand upon.

In the preface to the encyclical he notes that after the Cuban Missile Crisis in 1963, at a time of great danger in the Cold War, Pope John XXIII wrote the famous peace encyclical, *Pacem in Terris*. Francis describes his letter as a similar initiative. My comment on this comparison is meant to stress the significance of *Laudato Si'*.

The Catholic Church had taught and written about war and peace for well over a thousand years when *Pacem in Terris* appeared. But that encyclical put Catholic teaching on peace on an entirely new foundation. I believe that while Francis is not the first Pope to address the environment, he's raised the understanding of its significance for Catholics and for the world to an entirely new level. This encyclical will be seen, I believe, as the basis for Catholic engagement on the care of our common home for this century. The characteristics of the letter place it solidly in the Catholic social tradition. Pope Francis uses the resources of Revelation with extensive citations and reflections from Hebrew and Christian scriptures. He also joins these biblical themes with philosophical rigor and with an extensive use of the scientific analysis which has been at the heart of the environmental debate. Again, a quote from a very secular source is interesting. *The Washington Post* commented on the letter this way: "In his masterful grasp of the science behind climate change, the pontiff unmasked himself as a political wonk."

A final link of the encyclical with a prior Catholic teaching is Pope Francis' stated intention in his preface. He says, "I urgently appeal then for a new dialogue about how we are shaping the future of this planet. We need a conversation that includes everyone. Since the environmental challenge we are undergoing and it's human roots concern and affect all of us."

This call for dialogue echoes one of the principal statements in Vatican II's *Pastoral Constitution on the Church in the Modern World*. There the Council stated that the best way for the Church to show respect for the world was to enter into dialogue with it. Moving beyond the general character of the encyclical, I wish to lift up for consideration two sections of it.

First, in Chapter Two, the Holy Father offers a reflection on which he calls the Gospel of Creation. That is a fascinating, I would say, original reflection. It is tightly written, with biblical, theological meditation on how believers can approach this question of our relation to creation. He calls on believers to think of a triad of relationships of each of us with God, our neighbor, and creation. While personalizing the question in this way, Francis always keeps in the forefront of his definition of the environmental issues the social dimension of our existence. We face this problem as a global human community, even though decisions about it are made often through sovereign states, as was the case at the recent Paris summit of the United Nations. In the midst of his theological reflection, Pope Francis makes an important commentary on the Christian tradition and the environment.

In the creation account in the Book of Genesis stands the human person, made in the image of God. The dignity of the person is at the heart of Catholic social teaching and it lies at the center of the Pope's encyclical. But he goes on to point out that the Genesis mandate to the person, to exercise dominion over the earth, has at times been interpreted without proper restraint. Hence, in some discussions of the environmental challenge, Christians are seen as part of the problem. The Pope goes on to acknowledge that we Christians have at times incorrectly interpreted the scriptures. But, he says, today we must forcefully reject the notion that our being created in God's image and being given dominion over the earth justifies absolute dominion over all other creatures. In his own direct style of speaking, the Holy Father says, We are not God. The earth was here before us, and has been given to us. In interpreting the idea of our dominion over creation, the key idea is stewardship. We are to think of ourselves as the stewards of God's creation, so dominion must always be exercised within religious and moral limits. Thus, we will be good stewards of what God has entrusted with us, to us, His own work of creation. The idea of balance and the exercise of stewardship brings the encyclical to the moral core of the Pope's message. The moral argument about the environment runs through the entire encyclical. It is particularly found in Chapters Three and Four, entitled, "The Human Roots of the Ecological Crisis and Integral Ecology." I invite and urge you to read Francis' powerful indictment of human activity and the need for a true personal and social conversion. I will only summarize it here.

The premise of the Pope's approach, a theme he repeats again and again, is that all things are connected. One of the principal reasons the encyclical has received such praise from diverse quarters is that the Holy Father has provided a moral foundation for others to use in addressing this global crisis. He specifically connects two ideas, poverty and ecology. We have, he argues, not two different questions, but one large challenge. We must confront the environmental crisis because it threatens us all. In addition, the poor will suffer the greatest effects from a failure to address the environment. As Professor Oreskes nicely summarizes about the encyclical's moral arguments, the core of the argument is that because human dignity finds its roots in our common Creator, caring for our fellow citizen and caring for the environment are the same thing. Respect for creation and respect for human dignity are two aspects of the same idea. The Holy Father's moral critique of the cause of environmental degradation rests squarely on human choices. Or, as he puts it, the human roots of the ecological crisis. Once again, this argument runs through much of the encyclical. His primary purpose is not so much to allocate blame as to identify new and neater ways of changing how we think and act. The stress again lies on moral limits—how we set limits onto major dimensions of our common life, technology, and the markets.

My judgment is that he is not simply against either or both of these institutions of modernity. Rather, he sees both in need of moral direction. Neither technology nor the markets have their own inner ethic. Moral limits to guide the use of both are part of what social morality is about within nations, and among nations. In both cases, a basic criterion in deciding how to think about the intersection of ecology, technology, and the markets is their impact on the poor at every level of social life. The Holy Father does not propose his own singular, moral solution. Again, he invites dialogue across many sectors. Science, politics, business, finance, and at every level of life, local, national, and global. The Holy Father's moral analysis of the environment and poverty lies in this encyclical as the longer social economic teaching of the Catholic social tradition.

It also opens multiple questions for further discussion and examination of two issues—poverty and the environment—which run from the local to the global, and which are also inter-generational questions. The U.S. discussion and decision-making on these questions will spread out over space and time. Among the many compelling characteristics of *Laudato Si'* is the scope of the Holy Father's vision and words. He joins God and each person. Persons in community and social relationships, faith and reason, science and religion, economics and justice at every level of life. And he holds all together the three relationships he identified at the beginning of his encyclical: God, persons, and nature.

It's not surprising, therefore, that his concluding chapter is on spirituality and education. He opens saying that many things have to change course, but it is we human beings, above all, that need to change. The Holy Father describes the change needed as a cultural conversion involving how we think, how we see, and how we act faced with the double challenge of poverty and the environment. Throughout the encyclical he has used the resources of faith and reason, the best of theology and the best of science. He has spoken across lines to believers and humanists, to rich and poor, to climate skeptics and committed conservationists. In his concluding words, he focuses on those for whom faith is an abiding dimension of life. In this section, he reflects on how faith sheds light on all dimensions of reality and on all problems, however daunting the scope. His tone is meditative, reflective, and hopeful.

Having given us in one chapter the Gospel of Creation, he called on us in another chapter to an integral ecology. He leaves us with a sketch of how the sacramental life of faith can sustain a way of life with treasures in every dimension of God's creation. The sacraments, he reminds us, are a privileged way in which nature is taken up by God to become a means of mediating supernatural life. Through our worship of God, we are invited to embrace the world on a different plane. It is that embrace in which Francis hopes and prays that multiple communities of the world can adopt a different level of faith and reason. While his final reflections return to Catholics, and what he calls us to in belief and action, he is seeking to speak beyond the boundaries of the Church, and to save the common home that God has given us to share, to use, to protect, and to heal. Certainly, the encyclical is a great gift. Like the *Canticle of Brother Sun*, the encyclical is a hymn and a prayer. As a matter of fact, the encyclical ends with a prayer. And I would urge all of you to say that prayer, to study the encyclical, and to help our community to understand what a treasure this is, not just for our Church, but for the entire world. Thank you. [*applause*]

Cherico: Thank you so much. We do have a little bit of time for some discussion now, and I'm interested, first, in you, Dr. Sachs: you've read a tremendous volume of material in your life, addressing some of the concerns that the Pope is also talking about. I'm wondering, obviously: this is an ecclesial document, it's an encyclical, but it's clear that he's talking about our common home. He's looking to an audience that's broader than the Church itself. I'm wondering what, from your vantage point, you see as the most original contributions of the encyclical on the economy and environment and society in general? Things in which you are very well-versed in already.

Sachs: I think maybe it would be helpful just to say a word about the preparation of the encyclical, because it was amazing. Of course, the real preparation was Pope Francis writing the encyclical, which we didn't see; but for three years the Pontifical Academy of Sciences and the Pontifical Academy of Social Sciences worked very, very hard at bringing the world's top scientists and top development analysts to the Vatican for very serious and deep reflection on these issues. And I want to emphasize this because it's an amazing phenomenon. It's a unique phenomenon. There is no other world religion right now that works in this manner at all. There's a world-renowned scientific institution which I was privileged to be part of many meetings for three years, where top Nobel laureates, top analysts at one meeting, and the world's mayors were brought to the Vatican. At another, the world's top climate scientists, at yet another, religious leaders from across faiths came. So I think the process is phenomenally interesting, serious, and important, which is that a lot of work goes into this, in the Church. Science is not viewed as some outside extraneous matter; how could it be? It's viewed as completely integral to even the underlying morality of paying attention to science; it's fundamental. It can't be in contradiction with the moral questions in general, and that's why this encyclical is seamless between the science, the theology, and the guidance that it gives, which I think is unmatched in any other such text that I know.

But it doesn't come easily and it's not only the work of Pope Francis; it's the nature of how the Church is working right now. It's the empowerment of the Pontifical Academy of Sciences and the Pontifical Academy of Social Sciences, and the brilliant chancellor of those institutions, Bishop Marcelo Sánchez Sorondo. The idea that Pope Francis really encouraged those institutions to bring the science, study the problem, analyze the problem—it's so beautifully and seamlessly reflected in this, but it didn't come just out of nothing. I think that the process is extremely important to understand, because that's part of the gift. Such hard work went into this from so many different directions, and Pope Francis was the inspiration, because you go to the Vatican in part because it's so thrilling to see the moral call. And so from every faith, every top scientist, they say, *Yes, of course; what can we do to help?* The idea that these facts are put in such a powerful moral language is the inspiration that pulls all of this together.

Cherico: Thank you. To me, one of the interesting juxtapositions in the encyclical is this exclamation of praise that starts it, and this tremendous joy and enthusiasm—and then to go on and talk about some great issues of concern. The evangelical dimension that you see in the encyclical itself is interesting, and then also in the reception that it received. I'm wondering, Cardinal O'Malley, if you could speak a little bit about the pastoral concerns that you see at the heart of *Laudato Si'*.

O'Malley: Well, first of all, for me as a bishop, and for priests and religious educators, it's a wonderful opportunity to be able to present the Church's Magisterium to young Catholics, who very often have never read an encyclical or would not know what one was, and for them to realize that the Church is just as passionate about this theme that is so important to them, and isn't just a political stance but an ethical and a faith position. I think that, pastorally, it's a great opportunity for us to help our young people understand the great treasures of the social doctrine of the Church, the social gospel of the Church which is, I always say, one of our greatest secrets, because so many Catholics are unaware of the extraordinary teachings of the Church on human dignity, economic justice, racism; a whole series of social issues that touch our daily lives.

So for us it's a pastoral opportunity. Certainly, the pastoral concern of the Holy Father in writing this is to help form a world where there's a sense of unity and community. Where we are together in dealing with the problems of humanity. Of course, he threads throughout the encyclical the question of poverty. If any of you have ever been in parts of the world where there is practically no water, and to see how people are eking out an existence while those of us in the First World just turn on the spigot or go to the corner and buy a bottle of this water—for many people this would be such a luxury. The Holy Father's emphasis is on trying to call people together to look for the world's problems, the problems of humanity. The Jewish tradition has a beautiful expression. They talk about *Tikkun Olam*, "repairing the world." Well, this is what it's about, but repairing the world together, because if we don't do it together it's not going to work. The fact that the Holy Father cites the Ecumenical Patriarch Bartholomew and so many other religious traditions is an important indication of how the Holy Father is trying to get us to reach out and to work together for our common home.

Sachs: One of the magical aspects of these meetings, which were called by Cardinal Turkson, who directs the Pontifical Council for Justice and Peace, is that there was a meeting about climate science in the morning, then, in the afternoon, with the same participants, there was another meeting and the discussion turned to the questions of human trafficking and the excluded modern forms of slavery. At the beginning, the scientists and the community practitioners weren't quite sure why these were together, and what was the point about having these two sessions. But you saw the magic; that this was really about integral questions, and the climate scientists who study solar radiation, and how it's being affected by greenhouse gases and then listening to the change in the communities of the poorest of the poor, and what the implications were, and the feedback from the development practitioners back to the sciences was part of the magic of this. This is really the message, as you said, Cardinal, this is such a holistic and integral vision, and everybody feels empowered by it because of that. Just the design of putting people into these questions together has the effect of inspiring all parts of this discussion.

Cherico: That's really interesting, because there's this unity of thought that you're referring to in the encyclical; this connection, this common home, this connection between, say, natural ecology and human ecology. You were commenting earlier on the difficulty for many people in understanding the reality of life for the very poor. Do you think that's one of the concerns? I mean that repeatedly in the encyclical, the Pope refers to the disproportionate difficulties that the poor face in terms of ecological degradation. Do you think part of this is an attempt by him to try to get people to understand the nature of poverty, and to try to make this a more pressing concern to people for whom the poor are actually invisible in many ways?

O'Malley: The Holy Father so often talks about economic justice and the problems that poverty creates for the family, for women, for children, for the elderly. But here, he's going beyond that and saying, We're concerned about the poor, but if we're concerned about the poor, then we're going to be concerned about doing something around the environment because this is what is drastically affecting their lives and causing so much suffering. I think for a lot of people this was a concept they hadn't thought about, and the Holy Father certainly is emphasizing it here. Right from the beginning of his pontificate he's talked so much about economic justice, and even connected that with the gospel of life. But here he's going into some root causes, and the suffering of the poor and the degradation of the planet are certainly among them.

Sachs: Could I read a paragraph that I think is wonderful? And I'm going to make an advertisement for our program at Columbia. In paragraph 139 he says, "Nature cannot be regarded as something separate from ourselves, or as a mere setting in which we live. We are a part of nature, included in it, and thus in constant interaction with it. Recognizing the reasons why a given area is polluted requires a study of the workings of society, it's economy, it's behavior patterns, and the way it grasps reality. Given the scale of change, it is no longer possible to find a specific discreet answer for each part of the problem. It is essential to see comprehensive solutions which consider the interactions within natural systems themselves, and with social systems. We are faced not with two separate crises, one environmental and the other social, but rather with one complex crisis, which is both social and environmental. Strategies for a solution demand an integrated approach to combating poverty, restoring dignity to the excluded, and at the same time protecting nature."

This is the philosophy—here's my advertisement—we're trying at Columbia to introduce the concept of sustainable development as a new intellectual field, which also has that moral framework and is an integrated economic, social, and environmental analysis. We're trying to show that these integrated systems can be studied together and studied within a moral frame. I don't know if my colleague Bob Pollack is here—is Bob here?

Cherico: I don't think he was able to make it.

Sachs: Bob is one of the leaders of this effort, and we love this encyclical because we could put it in the recruiting brochure to explain the idea that we need an integrated vision. I want to give one U.N. advertisement as well, because as you know, we don't hear enough, really, about the wonderful things that the U.N., as a crossroads of the world, can do on the positive side. Not only did the world leaders adopt a climate agreement, but they adopted sustainable development goals. I always give a homework assignment: go home, look them up, and know them, because they are the global goals for cooperation for the coming generation. They've been adopted by all one hundred and ninety-three governments. They follow Pope Francis' call for an integration of the economic, the social, and the environmental. You will not be surprised to know that the Holy See made very important contributions to the formulation of the sustainable development goals, including the call to end modern slavery, which is one of Pope Francis' passionate calls to the world, and that became part of the U.N.'s call as well.

This integral view, which is at the heart of this encyclical, is being taken up, and I think that it is an extremely fruitful way for us to get out of this trap that we're in.

Cherico: Thank you. We appreciate your plug. Both of you have spoken about the encyclical in light of the longer Catholic social tradition, and also as a sort of personal call to transformation on an individual and social level. Pope Francis has often contrasted quite sharply with his predecessor. And it's interesting that in the encyclical he doesn't quote Benedict very frequently, but there are a couple of key moments that I found very interesting on that front. Early on, Francis notes that we have forgotten that man does not create himself. He quotes Benedict as saying, "Where we ourselves have the final word, where everything is simply our property, and we use it for ourselves alone, the misuse of creation begins when we no longer recognize any higher instance than ourselves, when we see nothing else but ourselves." Later on in the encyclical, at a more critical transition point, he again quotes Benedict: "The external deserts in the world are growing as the internal deserts have become so vast." And Francis refers to an ecological conversion, and the need for this ecological conversion. "Whereby the efforts of believers' encounter with Jesus Christ become evident in their relationship with the world around them."

I'm wondering if you could just say a few final remarks about the connection between this sort of internal desert and the loss of a sense of transcendence, with the more general social problem that we see before us, and whether or not you want to speak to it on a spiritual level.

O'Malley: First, to comment on Pope Benedict. They brought out a volume of Pope Benedict's teaching on ecology—I don't know if the professor has seen that or not, I'll try to get it. It's a very interesting work. But St. John Paul II also often talked about ecology and environment. There's been sort of a crescendo that has led up to Pope Francis, and certainly *Laudato Si'* is coming out of a very robust tradition, and has the great advantage of being a landmark encyclical. It's the first time that this has been dealt with as a single issue in the Church, and Pope Francis has raised it up in people's minds. I think if you ask parish social justice committees to give you a list of all the issues that the Church is concerned about, a lot would not include ecology, unfortunately. But after *Laudato Si'*, that cannot happen. Certainly, the Holy Father has invited us to see creation from a faith perspective. We cannot see wealth and natural resources simply as economic entities, but as parts of creation. There's a certain sacredness to it, and a connectedness. As the professor already indicated, the Catholic social teaching is that there is a social mortgage on all wealth. That is, the goods of the earth are to support everyone on the planet and must be shared; we have a role as stewards. I think that this theme of the Holy Father is a very important one, that we cannot look upon creation simply as something disconnected from God and disconnected from us. I think the triad the Holy Father talks about—God, people, and creation—is very, very important, and elevates creation. St. Francis saw everything in creation as a brother and a sister, be it the sun or the moon or the animal. We all have the same Creator and thus a relationship exists because of that.

Cherico: Well, I think we have to end there this evening. On behalf of the New York Encounter, I want to thank you both, Dr. Sachs and Cardinal O'Malley, for a fascinating evening. [*applause*]

NEW YORK

CARRÓN

Longing for Freedom and Yet (Not) Afraid

A conversation with ***Fr. Julián Carrón****, President of the Fraternity of Communion and Liberation, and* ***Fr. Jose Medina****, National Leader of Communion and Liberation in America, on the role of freedom in the pursuit of human desire*

Introduction

"We all talk about freedom. But what is freedom and what is its origin? What does it have to do with desire and human fulfillment? A great deal of uncertainty surrounds these questions. As a result, we find ourselves progressively replacing personal risk and responsibility with rules, policies, and risk management directives. It is as if we were afraid of experiencing too much freedom, and thus willing to trade it for one of its many palliatives. We are approaching what T.S. Eliot predicted in his "Choruses from the Rock"-- a society that "constantly tries to escape from the darkness outside and within by dreaming of systems so perfect that no one will need to be good" or, in our case, free. But what if freedom were not something to be regulated but plumbed to its depths?

"We often think of freedom as the absence of bonds or the possibility to do our own things or what we like. But this is not what freedom is. Even experientially or psychologically we feel truly free not when we do what we like best but, more keenly, when we feel satisfied, when something satisfies us. ... What is it, then, that can satisfy us? What can the soul be satisfied with? It's relationship with the infinite!"
(Msgr. Luigi Giussani, *The Risk of Education*, The Crossroad Publishing Company, 2001)

Sunday, January 17, 2016

Medina: Good morning, everybody. Since many of you know who I am, I'm not going to present myself. I'm very happy to have the opportunity to present and to spend a few minutes with Father Carrón. Father Carrón is a very dear friend of us, a father to many of us. He's the leader of the movement Communion and Liberation since 2005, since the passing of Father Giussani. Before that, Father Carrón was a theology professor. But more than anything else I want to insist on this aspect here: a friend and a father to many of us. We are very thankful that you are here, Father Julián. We are truly thankful. We had the curiosity this year, thinking about the theme of the New York Encounter, "Longing for the Sea and Yet Not Afraid," to try to explore with you the topic of freedom, because freedom for us in the United States is a value that we hold very dear. We call this the Land of the Free, and much of our social debate is centered around freedom. It's not something that we are unfamiliar with. It is something that is important to us. I wanted to ask you, in a sense, a very simple question: Why do you think it's so? Why do you think that this freedom is so important?

Carrón: Good morning, everybody. I am very happy to be with you and to share with all of you this moment of dialogue with Father Medina. To answer this question, we need to think about our history, because from the beginning of modernity we can say that freedom has been considered the most precious thing. I remember a quotation of Cervantes' *Don Quixote*—I am Spanish, I have to quote my friend[*laughter*]—who exposed how our freedom is: "Freedom, Sancho, is one of the most precious gifts heaven gave to man." The most precious gift. The treasures under the earth and beneath the sea cannot compare to it. For freedom one can and should risk one's life. From the beginning of modernity—and Cervantes is one of the witnesses to this beginning—we can recognize that freedom in a particular moment of history has become one of the most precious gifts that human beings have, and impossible to compare with anything else. I can imagine that this is like somebody taking a ship and embarking on an adventure of entering the sea, looking for something that is unknown but deeply longed for. Without worrying that one is risking too much. Cardinal Ratzinger once said said that this high regard for freedom does not seem to have faith. In the consciousness of mankind today, said Cardinal Ratzinger, freedom is largely regarded as the greatest good there is, after which all other good things have to take their place. Nowadays, this good is valued so much that it becomes the measure of everything. Cardinal Ratzinger goes on to say that this Enlightenment culture is substantially defined by the rights to liberty. At a certain point, it's liberty that is a fundamental value and the criterion of everything else. This is the consideration of freedom for our culture, for our environment, in the way our children feel about themselves, or our colleagues, or the husband and wife. Freedom. At the same time—and this is what strikes me more nowadays—we are no longer at the beginning of this journey of freedom that was begun centuries ago; other men and women have already covered a lot of ground in the journey. Where has this brought us? That is the question.

I want to explain with a small fact the journey of freedom over the last centuries, a story that a friend of mine told me about some time ago. "This evening I went to the the house of two classmates who are engaged and are living together without being married. After dinner, I stayed for a long time to talk, and the question of whether to have children or not came up. At a certain point, she told me, 'I'll never bring a child into the world. Who am I, to condemn another poor wretch to unhappiness? I'm not taking on that kind of responsibility. I'm not taking on that responsibility.' And then she added, 'I am afraid of my freedom. In the best of these cases, it's useless, and in the worst, I can cause someone pain.'" What they hope for in life is to try to do the least damage possible.

How can we have arrived at this point? From longing for freedom as the most precious gift, to this fear of freedom.

Medina: If I may interrupt, there is an expression in American culture, on the young side of the American culture, and it's called "FOMO"—fear of missing out. Which is a malady, an illness that many people have, in that they want to remain open to all possible choices, and therefore, out of a fear of missing something beautiful, they cannot commit to any of them. As I was listening to you, it reminded me of this experience. We want the possibility, us Americans, the thing that we love the most is the possibility of having all choices in front of us; but this having all choices in front of us fills us with fear. We've been fighting for a false understanding of freedom, so that no one can tell me, "Don't do that"—but this doesn't give me freedom. This is what the expression means, "fear of missing out." So, how did we come to this point, in which we've gone from fighting for freedom to actively fearing it?

Carrón: That is the question that everyone has to face. Because otherwise we keep speaking of freedom outside of experience. Outside of this particular point in which we are now. Because the event that I told you about is not an exception; it's not somebody who has a sickness and needs to go to the psychologist. Rather, it's the expression of our culture. I was struck by the fact that Kafka, years ago, wrote that men are afraid of freedom and responsibility. This fear of missing out. Says Kafka, they prefer to hide behind the prison bars which they built around themselves. We prefer to protect ourselves in a prison because of this fear of freedom. What is the process, Father Medina asked, leading up to this point? Freedom became identified along the way as an absence of bonds, of ties. Freedom came to be an individualistic way of being in reality without any ties, without any kinds of bonds, with absolute autonomy.

We can read this in one of the latest novels by Jonathan Franzen, *Purity*. It's the story of a man and woman who decide to split up because their relationship has become a prison. He writes, "Andreas was pitying her for this, he was savoring his coming freedom. The sweet freedom of getting away with everything, of never having to see her...friend again, or never having another discussion, we could have spent ten years in prison." For them, the relationship was a prison. We have spent ten years together—that was our prison. Maybe we have served our sentence. And if freedom comes to mean liberating oneself from any kind of tie or constraint, then to literally be free a person will have to belong to no one.

During his recent trip to the United States, Pope Francis said there are no longer close, personal relationships. It's now a fact. There is no need for demonstration. There are no longer close personal relationships. The sense of loneliness is so widespread. Even when we are together in a group, no? This is a confirmation of the Pope's statement. There are no longer personal relationships. Not only that we don't have any, we don't want them! Because that would make me depend on him or on her, and this is something to consider as a sickness, something to be treated by a psychologist. And the Pope continues: today's culture seems to encourage people not to bond with anything or anyone. Not to trust. The most important thing, nowadays, seems to be following the latest string of activity, whatever the cost or consequences. And the cost will be high, and the consequences grave.

Medina: I'm interested in this point here. There's a journalist at an online news site, *The Huffington Post*, who a couple months ago wrote an article that I found intriguing. He interviewed a person—and this is something that happens often—who had decided to save enough money in order to live life on a perpetual vacation. And when I say a perpetual vacation, I mean enough money to actually go around the world, like a vagabond, and I thought—

Carrón: [*interrupts*] Without any ties.

Medina: And it was intriguing to me—

Carrón: [*interrupts*] This is their dream. [*laughter*] To go around without any ties, any relationships, this is the dream for many people today.

Medina: And the thing I found intriguing was the ending of the article, because this woman had been going around the world for three-and-a-half years, and had been interviewed by the journalist; but at the end, there was a question, the last question was: Will you settle down? Will you love? Because she would say, No, but I have deep relationships with people, I have love while I travel—but there was still a sense that this unbounded freedom, this vagabond style, was nevertheless not enough. Not even for the person who was interviewing and admiring her, no? We're willing to follow this, no matter the consequences, but we have a sense that there are consequences to this unbound, vagabond sense of longing for the sea but not going anywhere.

Carrón: This is the question that we need to discover. Not as a cultural debate, or enter into the books to look for it, but to discover from inside our own experience. Because a woman who is a vagabond for years—she has all the space, all the freedom, to do whatever she decides—but at the end, she had to verify it. At the end, she needed to judge. Is it enough or not? What are the consequences of this way of living? What are the consequences of this vagabond way of life? The consequences are clear. They become clear that the absence of ties and constraints is not enough. I didn't read this article, but it is not enough to be totally cut off. In fact, this lack leads to the atrophy and eventual paralysis of freedom, because freedom needs something Other, something different than myself. To set in motion my freedom I need something important to me to move my freedom. If I don't care about anything, my life is flat, it has atrophied. It is the paralysis of my "I."

Freedom needs to be motivated by something attractive, and for it to be fully realized it needs a sufficient reason, otherwise the trajectory of freedom will be aimless wandering. This person didn't find anything so beautiful, so crucial for his life, that he said, "This is it, my freedom is to adhere to this," because there is nothing new, nothing so crucial for her or for him, and keeps wandering as a vagabond now. Like Jack Kerouac said, we've got to go, and we're never going to stop going till we get there. Where are we going? I don't know. But we gotta go. We don't know, but we got to go! This is the world. Our ideal is to become more and more a vagabond. And the consequences are clear in this atrophy of the "I" and the reason identified by Dostoyevsky—because Dostoyevsky identified this experience of freedom in his time. Because this kind of concession of freedom is boredom. Everything is so boring now. It is quite possible that the modern age, which began with such an unprecedented outward flourishing of human activity, with this thirst and longing for freedom and activity, may end, as said Arendt, in this "deadliest, most sterile passivity history has ever known." We can see a lot of uneasiness around, a lot of activity, but at the same time without moving the center of the "I." Then the center of our "I," the real activity, is blocked. And this is the consequence, because we haven't found yet something that can awaken my "I" from the bottom of myself. What can move the deepest part of my "I"? Because otherwise we keep doing many superficial things as part of my "I," but in the center part, in the most crucial part, my "I" is blocked.

Medina: That sentence, it makes me think, even personally, how especially when one is young, one always perceives the other as the reason why I am not free. Like, I'm thinking about being a child and my father says, No, you cannot do that and I cannot wait to actually arrive and say, I'll be free when you are not here. But now, we are in this situation in which, pretty much, you can do whatever you want. It's like, the doors of the prison are open, and then it's like, Go! And you go out there, and you're like, um...

Carrón: This is what our freedom is about. This is the moment in which we are living freedom. It's not at the beginning, it's not in that moment in which somebody frustrated us not to do something, no. Everybody can do what they want. But you have to discover that this is not enough.

Medina: But how do I discover what it is to be free? If I understand—and I understand very well in my personal experience—and I understand that I'm not free simply because I'm unbound, because I can choose to do what I want. And this, I think, is a great challenge to our American culture. That freedom does not coincide with equality, with choice. I can choose whatever I want, but I'm not free. So my question is: How do I discover what makes me free?

Carrón: At this point we are at a paradox, in that we can discover all of this through freedom. Because many times somebody comes, they'll say to you, But that's in the past, I will tell you what makes you free. But it doesn't work today. This kind of attitude. Why? Because along the way we have discovered that the way in which we can identify what moves our freedom is only known by some kind of imposition by somebody else. The Church, the state, the parents, the master in the schools, whatever. But we need to discover what is able to move the center of myself for freedom. And this is one of the things that has really surprised me in reading Don Giussani. The human person, said Giussani, as a free being, cannot be fulfilled, cannot reach his destiny except through freedom. And this can be a scandal for many people. I will tell you what made you free. No. Even the discovery of what makes us free is made only through freedom. Because "the human person as a free being cannot be fulfilled, cannot reach his destiny, except through freedom," reaching destiny. Continued Giussani, "Now if reaching destiny, fulfillment, is to be free, freedom must 'play a role' even in it's discovery, for if the discovery of this destiny, this ultimate meaning were automatic, then this destiny would no longer be mine."

For there are many times we can impose on one another some kind of will, some kind of idea, some kind of truth, but that doesn't mean that this truth becomes his or her truth. It does not become mine, my truth, because I can recognize something, mine, only through my freedom. The human person, concluded Don Giussani, is responsible before his destiny, because this is the fruit of his freedom. And this is the reason religious freedom is so important, to discover more and more consciously the importance of freedom of religion. The Church at the Vatican Council explained very well the relationship between freedom and truth. In a speech addressed to the Roman Curia in 2005, Cardinal Ratzinger stated that religious freedom is an intrinsic consequence of the truth. Not that religious freedom is a consequence of a failure to convince people that Christianity is the best for the human. "Given that we didn't convince people about the truth of the Christian religion, at least we can save the freedom of religion." No. Cardinal Ratzinger, or Pope Benedict XVI said, "This is an intrinsic consequence of the truth that cannot be externally imposed but that the person must adopt only through the process of conviction."

This is a crucial point. Religious freedom is the consequence of an awareness of the nature of the truth, and religion should be freedom and truth. Truth cannot be externally imposed, but must be embraced and adopted only in freedom, said the Pope.

He offered an example. Martyrs of the early Church died for their faith in God who was revealed in Jesus Christ. Martyrs died for their faith. But at the same time, and for this very reason, they also died for freedom of conscience. And the freedom to profess one's own faith, not in opposition to the state, but as a basic right of the human being. The Second Vatican Council, defining the relationship between freedom and truth, has helped us to have a right relationship between freedom and truth. Because it is only through freedom that we can discover the real nature of the truth. It belongs to the nature of the truth that can be discovered only through freedom.

Medina: Which is a very challenging statement due to, in part, when we think about religious freedom we are thinking that the state allows us to be, to do what we want.

Carrón: This is a part.

Medina: Which is a part. But you are introducing almost a vision, or an image of the Church as the great custodian of my freedom; and furthermore, you are saying that I cannot know or reach the truth if not through freedom. So I guess at this point the question that I have is: How can we today discover the truth through freedom?

Carrón: This is a very important question. It can allow us to introduce Giussani's conception of freedom. Giussani said, "How do we come to know what freedom is?" Words, freedom, love, reason. "Words are signs with which a person identifies a specific experience: the word *love* singles out a certain experience, as does the word *freedom*." As Father Giussani always taught, the first step to becoming aware of the meaning of the most important words in life is to look at our experience. When do we feel free? This is the starting point. And we need to come back to our history, to our experience, and to look for some moments in our life in which I can identify what happened in the moment that I felt free. You gave the example of longing to go out to a party her friends are throwing. Her father won't let her, and the girl's disappointment and anger are the unmistakable signs that she doesn't feel free. The starting point is a normal experience. The moment in which somebody has felt suffocated, or has felt free. From this example, Giussani said, we feel free when we see a desire satisfied. When I can fulfill my desire, I feel myself free when I can fulfill, satisfy my desire. The experience of freedom is the satisfaction I will have. Therefore, they mediate a distinct impression of freedom which is all we have, this idea that to be free is to do whatever I feel like. However, what is the problem, why in this social context in the world we are talking about, everybody has to do whatever he feels like? He's not free. This is our problem. What is the nature of the desire that he's not completely satisfied? Because in our answering of this question we aren't recognizing, we're not focusing on what is really the nature of the desire. It's impossible to recognize when this desire could have been satisfied.

And Giussani continues, "Experience indicates that freedom presents itself to us as a total satisfaction, a complete fulfillment of the self as perfection." But the question is, What is the nature of our desire? Saint Augustine identified the question in three words. *Quod anima satis*; what will truly be enough to satisfy the desire of the heart? What is *quod anima satis*? Because all of us have the experience of the Italian author Cesare Pavese, who finally attained the crucial success in his life by receiving the prestigious Strega prize. The most prestigious literary award in Italy. After receiving it he asked: And now what? What can I do?

Medina: I personally think this is a very crucial moment because the "and now what" is what leads us to something else. So what is it that satisfies, like what is the meaning of this experience of this satisfaction? Because I think that otherwise we are like our vagabond friend, as you were saying before, going around the world, saying "And now what?" Okay, I go somewhere else. What do you learn from this point here?

Carrón: What do we learn from this point? Because this is the question. Why am I not completely satisfied in the most important moment of my success, when I can reach what I could consider impossible to arrive at? But in many times, life answered to my desire. But it is not enough. What does it teach us about ourselves, about the nature of our desire? I cannot find another way of expressing the nature of the desire than what the Italian poet, Giacomo Leopardi, summarizes in these phrases: the desire that we discover in ourselves and the reason because we are not completely satisfied is that our desire is infinite. Whatever word we can use. If somebody doesn't like infinite, we can use another word. Endless desire, greater desire, immense desire, whatever word, we don't want to waste our time in discussion about the word infinite. We discovered ourselves with our desire, that even with the most important success, there is nothing there for us.

Giacomo Leopardi said it's precisely this boundless horizon of our desire that makes us, because we have this immense, endless desire. We can "accuse things of insufficiency and nothingness, and suffer weakness and emptiness, yet boredom." Because it is not enough. But this is not a problem because I am sick; I am a human being. I am a person who is constituted by this immense desire, like the vagabond, without limit. But for many people, perceiving the insufficiency of everything and suffering weakness or emptiness, it is a curse in life. It's like a condemnation, a sickness, a prison; but for Leopardi, it is the sign of the greatness of the human being. We are so great that we are this enormous desire that nothing can satisfy completely. In fact, we can perceive the insufficiency of things precisely because we have the criteria of judgment built inside of us. We cannot be human without this criterion, this tool, that allows us to judge what is expedient: we can call it infinite desire, or simply the heart. If you don't want infinite desire, you can use heart. Not to be used as a certain feeling, but a judgment. The problem of our life is that our heart can't be contented with anything else than with something that corresponds to all the longing or the thirst for fulfillment.

And we can go wandering around the world, and study all kinds of philosophy, or belong to another kind of religion, but if there is not something that can correspond to our desire, it will not be enough to move our freedom along the way. And for this reason, after awhile, because it is not enough, there is no attractiveness to become mine forever, I need to change, I need to wander again.

Medina: But I see that and I see this is part of the human journey, in a sense, that even my vagabond friend—at this point we are friends—still longs, as the title of the New York Encounter this year says, longs for something. Longs for someone. Even in an unbound life there is enough information ultimately to say: But I need to be in relationship with someone. And I hear you when you say that we are made for this someone great who we long for. But it is, I would say, almost inhuman to remain in this position without being able to see this someone that I long for. Meaning ultimately, my friend, you were saying before, speaking about freedom, that I can only be free if I am attracted to someone. So, ultimately, how am I going to be able to be free if the Mystery remains a Mystery?

Carrón: First of all, the point to identify, the only answer to my infinite desire is the Infinite, is the Mystery. Because everything else is too small. For this reason I always remain unsatisfied. It's impossible that I can overcome my wandering around, my vagabond issue. We can say this, in our human experience. Everybody is longing for love, and to be loved. We don't know before meeting the person, Who is it? It's the reason we keep wandering, because we don't know. What is the moment in which we can be attracted? When this person, whose face I didn't know before, is revealed to myself and I have her before me, in front of me. And I am so attracted that my wandering is finished because I met her, or met him. This is the way in which we can understand why it's impossible to be attracted to something that doesn't coincide with this Mystery, because it's not enough. And we, after awhile, become bored with this thing, and we start to look for another thing that can be new, attractive.

The only possibility is that something happens in life. I keep wandering around unless God visits me. I keep wandering, looking for something else that can fulfill my desire unless the Infinite visits me. What is the visitation of Christ, of the Mystery? The Incarnation? The Incarnation is the Infinite became flesh, finite. And in that moment, when people encounter him —they were so attracted that John and Andrew remained Jesus' friends forever. The thing is to be there at the beginning for awhile, making a lot of mistakes; for that doesn't matter. But they were so attached to Jesus that they remained faithful, remained friends, because where can I go? No other has attracted me like you. No other has moved the inner part of my "I" other than yourself, other than you, Christ. We can discover this in the middle of reality, like John and Andrew or the disciples, through freedom. The last thing that John and Andrew could have imagined the day they met him was that something like this could happen, but it happened. It really happened and they were there, the most important day of their life. They remembered the hour, the time, the precise moment because genuine freedom, said the Pope, is the fruit of a personal encounter with Jesus. It is the fulfillment of desire. But this is an experience, it's not a theory, a lesson, it's not a speech, it's not a preaching. If somebody doesn't have this kind of experience, it's impossible to convince him that this is true, because this happens through freedom, in a personal encounter, in which the truth that is a person, not an abstraction, the truth became flesh. And we can recognize that this is the truth because no other is capable of satisfying my life like him.

Medina: And with this I want to close, even though I would like to continue. Because ultimately, to this woman who chooses to go for years on vacation looking for someone, looking for something—you are basically saying the only possibility of truly experiencing freedom is not that you get to choose every morning what you want to do; it's that you have an experience of satisfaction. And that experience of satisfaction is only possible if the Mystery, this Infinite that we desire, that is an expression of who we are, makes Himself present to me. And yes, you recall the Gospels and the story of Jesus and Peter, but the only salvation for my friend, for myself, for all of us, is whether that experience happens now. We say that the Church is the place in which the Christian event continues to happen, but how? How can we tell?

Carrón: In a witness. This experience. The only possibility for our wandering man who is around the world; what other possibility does he have? Only to be open; to be open to this possibility, because he has this thirst for fulfillment and nobody can content himself without this fulfillment. So, the question is that we can be so open, so willing to recognize when this happens. This can't happen if we don't meet in the middle of the reality, along the way, in the place that we could have imagined before, like John and Andrew, present, so I can see fulfilled what I am looking for. This is a witness. Giussani said, and we can finish with this: "What is missing now is not the verbal or cultural repetition of the announcement, a doctrine, or a set of rules, or a set of values. Everything is sufficient. What is missing is not a verbal or cultural repetition of the announcement, or the truth. People today perhaps unknowingly await the experience of an encounter with people for whom the fact of Christ is such a present reality that the life is changed. A human impact is what can shake people today." A human impact. Not only is it a value, not only a doctrine, not only a preaching; a human impact is what can shake people today, an event that echoes the initial event in which we can find the initial event now in the present. Otherwise, the Christian event is dead. Something that remains in the past, that only lists doctrines and traditions but without any possibility of awakening the desire now and fulfilling it.

Medina: Thank you.

ng for the Sea and yet Not Afraid
PISCITELLI
SANCHEZ

Longing for the Sea...and Leaving the Harbor

Eyewitness accounts of stories of immigration and welcoming with ***Msgr. Ronald Marino****, Vicar for Migrant and Ethnic Apostolates Diocese of Brooklyn;* ***Giulio Piscitelli****, Photographer; and* ***Stephen Sanchez*** *(moderator), Principal, Our Lady of Mount Carmel School, New York*

Introduction

The current lively debate about immigration often overlooks that our country has been and is built by immigrants. The question is not how we face immigration, but how we face immigrants, real human beings with needs, talents and expectations. People do not go through the trauma of uprooting themselves and their families for frivolous reasons. Evidence mounts that the present global migration can be explained by several key factors. Poverty, hunger, violence, disregard of human rights and the search for economic and intellectual fulfillment unavailable at home are among the root causes of this exodus. Any approach to migration which ignores the root causes of this phenomenon, thus nurturing an ideological attitude, is short-sighted and will ultimately fail. On the one hand, neither abstract legalism nor nativism are adequate responses to the question posed by the presence of immigrants. On the other hand, a naive, universalistic openness to immigration, which is forgetful of the profound and complex challenges which a society hosting and welcoming the immigrants has to face, is also not enough.

What can overcome the distress of leaving your own country? What can surmount the mistrust to embrace an entirely new way of living? And what can defeat the fear of welcoming a stranger in your home country?

Saturday, January 17, 2015

Sanchez: Good afternoon and thank you for joining us. How could we talk about the journey across the sea without actually talking about those who journeyed across the sea amidst all sorts of fears that have been overcome? We thank you for joining us here as we look at "Longing for the Sea and Leaving the Harbor," and the experience of immigrants all across the world. Here to share this with us are two fascinating people, both for their breadth of experience and their insight.

Monsignor Ronald Marino is a priest of the Diocese of Brooklyn, Episcopal Vicar for Migrant and Ethnic Apostolate, and has over twenty-five years of experience working for immigrant families in the Catholic Migration Office, which he started in the Brooklyn diocese and served for seventeen years. He was ordained a priest in 1973 after having obtained his Bachelor of Arts degree from Cathedral College in Douglastown, New York, and has a Master of Divinity degree from Immaculate Conception in Huntington. He continued his post-graduate studies and obtained a Master of Science in Education Counseling from St. John's, and in 1994 he founded Resources, Inc., a nationally-recognized job opportunity program for immigrants. He is frequently called upon to speak on immigrant pastoral issues, both nationally and internationally.

Giulio Piscitelli is a native of Italy and a professional photographer of not a long experience: he started in 2008, but has an incredibly fascinating vision. He earned his degree in Communication Studies, and after graduation began working with the Italian and foreign news agencies. His works are often exhibited both in Italy and abroad.

In 2012 he won a grant from the Magnum Foundation Emergency Fund for the continuation of his photographic project, *From There to Here*, focused on immigration in Italy. In 2015 he received the World Report Award for his extensive work on immigration. In addition to this project on immigration, he also has carried out photographic work in Syria, Afghanistan, Kosovo, the Sudan, Egypt, Kenya, Libya, Tunisia, and Ukraine. His reports were published by national and international newspapers and magazines such as *The New York Times*, *Espresso*, *Stern*, Newsweek, *Vanity Fair*, and *Time*, among others, so please join me in welcoming these two guests. Thank you. [*applause*]

Piscitelli: Thank you very much, I'm happy to be here, to give the possibility of sharing our experience. I'm sorry in particular for my English, my rusty English; probably it's not my best way to present my work.

Anyway, before we start to have this fast chat, I want to show you part of my work in a video that collects the main steps of my work in these last five years, on the roles of the refugees and migrants that try to reach the old continent.

[VIDEO]

This is my sixth year working on this topic. I started 2009, 2010, following the stories of the immigrants in Italy. It was my school and teacher. This topic was my teacher to stay alive in the world, because learning a lot and understanding the others—I wanted to understand the person. I started to follow the story in Italy and then enlarged my work to Tunisia after the fall of Gaddafi, because in that period more than 600,000 people fled Libya and, of course, a lot of these people arrived in Italy. In that period, I had one of the most important experiences in my life, because I decided to describe the trip of these people from the coast of Libya to Italy. I embarked with these people. I decided by myself to do this trip with them because I was curious as a journalist. It is the first thing for a journalist to be curious, to see with my eyes the dangers of these people, that these people have to face, and try to understand why these people decide to do this dangerous route. As I told you, it was one of the most important experiences in my life, because I saw for the first time the humanity of people who helped themselves to go, go over the difficulty of a trip like this. This trip taught me to look in another way at every topic and every problem that I'm going to take picture of. I also understood that, of course, the decision to move from your house, from your home, depends on different decisions. Sometimes you escaped from the bombs. The great part of the Syrians that are escaping in this period are escaping from one of the worst wars of the last twenty years. But a lot of people escaped from their house because there are no hopes. We can say that the first thing that moves a person to move is hope. Because in most of the situations like the Syrian situation, there are no other hopes. There are deaths, or the hope that you will not die during your route. There are other people, of course, who escaped from their place; a lot of people are not escaping from the bombs. A lot of people are escaping from the poverty.

This is not less important than to escape from the bombs, because we return to the same words, the hope, the hope to give yourself a better possibility to live in another place, to find a place where you can live in a better situation, like in the case of the Syrians or the Somalis. To find a place for your children. In my opinion, the different hopes are at the base of the movement of the great part of people who decide to leave their house, because in my view, your house could be golden, or it could be a shock, but it's always your house and it is difficult.

No one decides to leave his place without a reason. If we speak with the great part of the people who escaped from Iraq in 2005, the great part of these people will continue to hope to come back to their house, to their home. This is one of the great things I learned in my work, that the hope to find a better place, a place in peace, is the first thing for human beings in general. It is important, was important, that I saw that a great part of us, a lot of people here, have Italian roots, so we can understand, because during the Second War, the great part of our family moved to America, to Argentina because they just wanted to improve their life, escaping from poverty, not necessarily from the bombs. I tried to imagine what it means to escape from the bombs. There is nothing worse than to see your children in danger, to die under a bomb, under the rubble of a building; or worse, to see your children already dead. You start to hope to find another place. A lot of these people, and I'm not speaking about the Syrians, who have a faster way to get inside Europe in this moment, but a lot of people whose hopes are broken because they found in Europe not what they dreamed of. I mean, it's not easy to find another home in a foreign country. But they continue to hope. To hope for their sons. To hope for their children that the society that they decide to visit is the society that will give their sons the hope for a better life.

I conclude by saying that for me, this story, this project, changed my life as a human, as a journalist, because the enormous humanity of these years enlarged the possibility to understand better what I'm looking at and make me stronger, because it built in me the possibility to be critical in front of what I'm seeing. I'm speaking about, for example, the ongoing crisis about terrorism, so I'm critical about it, and I have to say that I'm critical because I saw the things I saw, that the people escape for a reason, and if we now are facing the lack of hopes of these people in Europe, I know why a lot of people decide to come back with a wrong decision—following, for example, Islamic State, or other kinds of radical cultures. Anyway, I hope that the rest of the people who are continuing to hope to find their path, that our society will open their eyes, and will change with this change of the cultures that are arriving in our society for a better way. I don't know. I'm thinking that we are facing an enormous changing in the U.S., in Europe, and the only fear that I have is that we are not ready to understand that the change passes through all these peoples. We have to be critical, and we have to be open to understand and see clearly that a society without this kind of changing is a society that will necessarily die, and that's what my work gave me. I'm transformed into a person that is open to the possibility that my society will change totally, radically, into something that I have never seen. Also, the people who are arriving are probably more ready than us, because they have already seen their culture and their society totally destroyed. They just have to hope that the next society can give them something more, and we have to participate in building society. I conclude to say that I'm continuing to hope that we will wake up from this dream that society is stuck; we don't want to be stuck. We need to change. Thank you and I hope I don't bore you too much. [*applause*]

Marino: Such powerful images that have to touch you. Such experiences that people had, still have, and unfortunately will continue to have. Things that you and I cannot ignore. Things that you and I can only learn from, and that's why I'm grateful for the invitation that was given to me to speak today, and I know that it was done because of my many years of having this unique privilege of working with immigrants, refugees, and their families. It is a great privilege to me to have been assigned to do this work in the name of the local church of the Diocese of Brooklyn. Please notice that I said *assigned*. Yes, it was simply out of obedience, not my choice, that I began this journey of mine.

Today in speaking about it to you, I want to speak about my "I." Not this one [*points to his eye*] but this one [*points to heart*]. Because I think as it was said before, we all learn from these experiences, and we are changed because of these experiences. And unless these two things happen, that we learn and we change, the experiences have no value except that they are sad stories that we can watch on television or see in the newspaper. At first I had my doubts. I had never worked with immigrants before and I really enjoyed being a parish priest. I didn't feel qualified, and I felt really inadequate. A priest working in an office was not my idea of being a priest. Now, years later, I recognize it as the action of the Holy Spirit in my own life, putting me in a boat and guiding me to find fulfillment and happiness in my own life.

The film in the photos that we have just seen gives a striking sense of the experience of people on the move. It didn't look easy, and it wasn't, and it still isn't. I won't begin by listing all the struggles and difficulties which I saw people facing as they arrived here. You can imagine them yourselves. Nor will I list hypotheses as to why they left their homeland, because they all come down to these: to live in freedom, to provide dignity for their family here and abroad, and to begin anew with hope.

Instead, I am tracing my own journey and reflections on what the Holy Spirit desired for me. I think it might be useful for all those who ask themselves the question in view of all the difficulties of these migrant peoples, What can I or should I do about it? Anyone with a Christian heart would be moved to want to intervene somehow. However, the same feeling of inadequacy takes over almost immediately. Offering—often rendering us helpless, but full of searching and hope. Maybe in hearing my reflections, you can avoid the mistakes I made in understanding God's will.

My first mistake was thinking that I had some special characteristics or gifts that made my bishop assign me to do this work. I was flattered, but I knew that basically I had no such special gifts. I knew nothing about immigration, and obeying my superiors simply meant going to an office every day and waiting for somebody to call with a question that I knew nothing about. "Should I go to law school?" I asked myself. What books should I read, since I was working in the first Catholic immigration office in the United States? There was no other model existing for me to learn from. The only other language I was any good at was Italian, and there were no Italian refugees here except CL members. [*laughter*]

Most newcomers knew Spanish, Chinese, Korean, Haitian, Creole, Polish, etc., but I didn't. So much for speaking to anyone or understanding them. You see, mistake Number One was not looking outside myself and forgetting that there was the possibility of a bigger plan afoot. I didn't trust this plan, because I felt inadequate in the face of the challenge before me. I kind of hid myself in my office at my desk, and made work, wrote memos, and answered the phone. I didn't pray for enlightenment or guidance from the Lord, but kept focusing on my own emptiness. In the meantime, the diocese was filling up with immigrants of every kind. I heard about them from the local pastors. They were filling up our Sunday Masses, not giving money in the collections. Wanting to celebrate saints and Madonnas which no one ever heard about. They were unaware of the English language. They were working off the books and sending their money home each payday, and being taken advantage of everywhere. The sense of inadequacy and frustration of the pastors quickly gave me a new sense of purpose, namely, to provide for them what they themselves could not provide. I began creating a parade of projects and programs which could be done at the local level. English classes run by my office. Job training programs run by my office. Legal assistance programs offered at community locations. Foreign language programs for priests, and many such other programs for which I am "famous."

My ministry began to have meaning. I discovered organizational talents I never knew I had, but still no "me." After about ten years of doing these kinds of things, raising funds for them, enrolling hundreds of immigrants in programs, and feeling very satisfied and appreciated, as evidenced by the many speaking engagements I was invited to, both here and abroad, I had a revelation. I was on a retreat doing some reading when I came across this sentence. "When you come into the presence of other cultures, and the poor, take off your shoes, because you will be walking on people's dreams, and more importantly, because God walked there first." Was I really walking in God's footsteps, or making my own paths? Was I ministering to immigrants, or looking to others to do it? While the programs were wonderful, I kept asking myself, Where is Christ? Am I following him, or leading others in my own footsteps? I got obsessed with this question, and had to find him or else I was only a Catholic social worker with the sacrament of Holy Orders to make me different from others.

Mistake Number Two was not looking for Jesus or seeing him in the immigrants and refugees I was serving. I was too far away from them to see him. I needed to put myself directly in their company and listen to them. Since evangelization is listening, not talking, I had to listen more. I had to be evangelized. Jesus said, "I was a stranger and you welcomed me."

On a visit to Rome, by chance I came across a book about the human face of Christ. It was in Italian and difficult for me to get through. Somehow, I knew what it spoke about, and what I needed to see in my work. I needed to experience what some people call, "the event." I needed that encounter with him somehow in the place where the Holy Spirit put me. I needed to realize that the desire in my own heart was not to be famous for what I could do, but for who I am in the eyes of the Lord. I began to see him everywhere, and in everything. I remember going into a church in Rome where the most boring homily was being given. [*laughter*] It only happens there. I looked around at the congregation. I could see that people were engrossed in praying for their own intentions, asking for help of all kinds from the Lord, crying, and in deep thought. The preacher seemed oblivious to all this. At the end of that Mass, I went to sit next to a man who looked very sad and had been crying. I began to ask him what was wrong but he didn't speak any language that I knew. He gestured a lot, and finally pulled out a picture of his family; he made me understand that he was there in Rome alone, and that they had been left behind. He had no one for himself. Unable to give him any of my usual words of wisdom, I just sat there next to him and prayed. After about twenty minutes he stood up, pulled me up, and hugged me, then he left. I was overwhelmed and sat right back down in the church and I said to myself, I finally saw the human face of Christ.

In what was the fastest nine-hour flight from Rome, I kept thinking about that incident and what it meant for my work with immigrants. I felt renewed in my priesthood. Angry at how blind I had been all these years. Determined to become a stronger advocate for the rights and dignity of immigrants and refugees, and never to lose sight of what I had seen on that church bench.

Once I realized this, I began to use my authority and reputation to speak about immigrants in this way. Immigration is a moral issue, not a political one. That is why we believe that it's morally wrong for families to be separated, because they cannot survive living together in their own country. It is morally wrong for people to die every day in the desert because there are no laws to allow them to come here legally. It is morally wrong to imprison asylum-seekers without due process of law. It is morally wrong to use people's—let people use their life savings to be smuggled by unscrupulous traffickers. It is morally wrong to force people to live in fear and hiding, while using their labor openly without fear of punishment for the employer. The human face of the migrants' situation turns the issue inside out. We must always discuss the root causes of people who are fleeing persecution, famine, and poverty. The Catholic Church has always taught that people have a right to live in dignity in the place where they were born. The Church has an immigrant policy, not an immigration policy. I also learned that other religions are part of God's plan for salvation. All migrants, though not necessarily religious in their own country, rediscover religion after they migrate, and hold on to it as their only consolation in their struggles.

In the experience of migrating for whatever the reason, people are in the process of finding meaning in their lives. This is theology in practice. They are not the objects of evangelization, but the subjects of it. That is why we must create a climate to remove fear and create trust. Our Holy Father recently said that people do not learn about the faith from a book, they long for it in their hearts. When people see people of faith, who really care about them and listen to them, they want to understand why. Why are they listening to me? Migrants hear important things with their eyes. Mother Teresa did not need to preach.

In summary, I could have spoken about individual people for whom the event of encountering Christ along the journey changed them profoundly. Migrants, after all, are the place where holiness and justice meet. They were still poor, they were still treated unjustly, they are still the victims of prejudice and violence, but something changed in them. How do I know? Because they allowed me to change. They showed me the face of Christ I had been looking for without even realizing it. I have left to your own imagination the stories and faces of the people I have met. My own heart aches when I see the hundreds of thousands of people still in boats, still making the journey, still longing. But I rejoice in the knowledge that people are waiting for them on the shores, whose own hearts will be changed when they arrive sooner or later. And if those people realize what they are waiting for, and who they are waiting for, the world will be a much better place for everyone. Thank you. [*applause*]

Sanchez: We have time for a question. Listening to each of you, the thing that strikes me is the question that I had before, and one that comes from a particular history. I was invited to moderate this talk, because my last name is Sanchez. [*laughter*]

I laughed when they said this, because my family has been on the same piece of land for four hundred years. We came with the Spanish conquest, and the country's changed, but we remained. All my life I've been around immigrants, I've worked with them here in the Archdiocese of New York, and I have a school in which seventy percent of my families are recent Mexican immigrant families. And the thing that strikes me when I see them, and when I think about their experience here, is what it means to call a place home. How does a foreign place become home? And even for those of us who are home, how does that shape and take root in the identity that we claim for ourselves as Americans or as Europeans, or whatever, particularly Mexicans, whatever particularly significant place we come from? I'll let Giulio answer first.

Pisctitelli: I think it is not an easy answer to say what is home, why you can feel home in a place. I have my personal answer that home is where my shoes are. And I think, of course, that answer will change, obviously, from one person to another. I mean to return to the Syrian refugees. For sure, all the men who escaped from Syria will never call home where we have to stay. Probably his son, or grandson, will call this, the new place home, because he is born there; he has never seen the home of his grandfather. But home is a mood, home is something that you feel where your heart is, where your heart is comfortable. Where there are your roots or not necessarily your roots, but something that you feel… family. I can use these words, but of course home is something that you feel, and probably for a person that has a house that is familiar, it is more easy to say what is home. Home is where my girlfriend is, where your mother, children, or wife is. But try to imagine what should be the answer from, I don't know, a young man from Somalia who lost his entire family, his entire house, his entire country, his entire culture, what is personal. Ask him, What is home? I tried to put my feet in his shoes and really, I don't have an answer. Home—I know what was my home, probably. I know what could be, what I would like to be my next home, but at the moment I don't know what is my home. I know what is my shelter, probably. So I think it depends.

Marino: I think the definition of home is a place where you feel like you belong. Whatever country you're in, whatever group you're with, once you know that you belong, then you are at home. And how you know you belong is when you feel people reaching out to make you belong. I remember I used to tell the pastors don't think that people are welcome in your parish just because you say they are. People are welcome when they say they are. Because they were doing things like Spanish bingo, and they were doing things like turkey drives, when people didn't eat turkey. They were doing all the American things in Spanish, or in Polish, and saying, "Look how my people are welcome: we made room for them on the parish council!" Geez. *I* don't even like to go to the parish council. [*laughter*]

So that's not it. That's not it. It's making people understand that they belong. They look for their food. It sounds stupid, but believe me, you hand them what they have been used to eating, what their mother only knew how to make, what they realize somebody went and found for them, you see a smile like you have not seen in a long time.

Company of other people, hospitality; not that you take a boatload of refugees, invite them to your basement to live, that's not it. Hospitality is something that shows there's room in your heart for people first. Then, there's room somewhere else. I think people would like me to say the thing that makes them feel at home is the faith. We can't speak like that anymore. What faith—the Muslim faith? The Orthodox faith? The Catholic faith? They are of all different faiths. But what is it about all those different faiths? It's the same God, who wants from them what he wants from us. And I think the more we can help them to be people of their own faith, the better off they are and will feel at home. So I have a very simple answer there. The belonging, making people feel like they belong, is probably the most important part of making someone feel at home.

Sanchez: I'd be remiss if I didn't say that when I was a kid, the first thing that made me want to understand what it meant to be an immigrant was a poem by Emma Lazarus that almost every kid memorizes in this country at some point, third or fourth grade. And I think that if we think of ourselves as a people who welcome immigrants, and not who develop policies on immigration, it rings true for us as well.

The New Colossus
By Emma Lazarus

Not like the brazen giant of Greek fame,
With conquering limbs astride from land to land;
Here at our sea-washed, sunset gates shall stand
A mighty woman with a torch, whose flame
Is the imprisoned lightning, and her name
Mother of Exiles. From her beacon-hand
Glows world-wide welcome; her mild eyes command
The air-bridged harbor that twin cities frame.
"Keep, ancient lands, your storied pomp!" cries she
With silent lips. "Give me your tired, your poor,
Your huddled masses yearning to breathe free,
The wretched refuse of your teeming shore.
Send these, the homeless, tempest-tost to me,
I lift my lamp beside the golden door!"

COUNTER

ZAKNOUN

“Your Love is Better than Life” (Psalm 62)

A testimony on the life of Christians facing terror and death in the Middle East by ***Archbishop Amel Nona****, exiled Chaldean Catholic Archbishop of Mosul, Iraq,* ***Fr. Pier Battista Pizzaballa****, Custodian of the Holy Land, and* ***Marta Zaknoun*** *(moderator), Journalist*

Introduction

“One of the most overwhelming human tragedies of recent decades is the terrible consequence that the conflicts in Syria and Iraq have had on civilian populations as well as on cultural heritage. Millions of people are in a distressing state of urgent need. They are forced to leave their native lands...There are many victims of this conflict: I think of all of them and I pray for all. However, I cannot fail to mention the serious harm to the Christian communities in Syria and Iraq, where many brothers and sisters are oppressed because of their faith, driven from their land, kept in prison or even killed. For centuries, the Christian and Muslim communities have lived together in these lands on the basis of mutual respect. Today the very legitimacy of the presence of Christians and other religious minorities is denied in the name of a ‘violent fundamentalism claiming to be based on religion’ Yet, the Church responds to the many attacks and persecutions that she suffers in those countries by bearing witness to Christ with courage, through her humble and fervent presence, sincere dialogue and the generous service in favor of whoever are suffering or in need without any distinction.” (Pope Francis, excerpt from the Address of the Participants of the Meeting organized by the Pontifical Council *Cor Unum* on the Iraqi-Syrian humanitarian crisis, September 17, 2015)

What is the situation of Christians today in Iraq, Syria, and other parts of the Middle East? In that situation, is it still possible to look for happiness

---

Sunday, January 17, 2015

without being dominated by fear and hatred? Can one look at people of a different religion or culture without distrust or indifference, but rather as an occasion to deepen one's own identity?

Zaknoun: Good afternoon, my name is Martha Zaknoun and I am a free-lance journalist. I was born and raised in Jerusalem and I currently live in Toronto. I'm very happy to be here with you today. Our encounter this afternoon is entitled "Your Love is Better Than Life," from Psalm 62. This encounter will turn our attention to the Middle East, a region often characterized by its state of turbulence and instability, and whose political contexts have increasingly affected us in a direct way over the last ten years. When in 2010 the first waves of the Arab Spring emerged, the world looked at them in awe, expecting the change that so many young people in that region were hoping would come about in their countries. It seemed like we were on the verge of the democratization that would spring from the emergence of a new mindset and the critical awareness of the citizens of those countries who wanted more freedom, equality, and an overall better life. The young generation of those nations was eager to generate a change. Following the fall of the long-established authoritarian regimes, fundamentalists and extremist Islamic groups seized the opportunity to deviate this moment of popular protest. Gradually, and across various Arab countries such as Egypt, Syria, and Yemen, just to name a few, the absence of the rule of law allowed for these ideologies to rise to the surface and gain ground, frustrating that initial, noble attempt and uprising with an ideological battle over power.

Soon enough, upheavals evolved to dissensions and violence, and several Arab countries witnessed an increasing sectarian violence that unfolded into full-fledged civil wars. Within that context, Arab countries have also witnessed various international military and political interventions. In the case of Iraq, however, the problem had begun long before, in 2003, after the fall of Saddam's regime. The conflict between Shiite and Sunni factions escalated, and with the absence of the rule of law there was a rise of the extremist groups, religious discrimination, and the persecution of Christians and other religious minorities increased. In the meantime, the ongoing sixty-eight year-long Israeli and Palestinian conflict seems to be ever more distant from a possible peaceful solution, with a recurrent escalation of violence between the two sides. Today, we are looking at the Middle East with dismay, at the hundreds of thousands of victims and millions of refugees and displaced people escaping from brutal wars that have created an unprecedented humanitarian crisis with four million refugees from Syria alone. We are seized by concern also when we look at our own experience with the expansion of extremism and violence into our cities of Europe and North America, the events in Paris being one of the more salient and dramatic examples of that. We find ourselves alarmed, disoriented, and often paralyzed by our fear. It seems that the media frenzy and the elaborate political discourses fall short, and they cannot pull us out of this state. If anything, they are more likely to add to our own confusion. Yes, this fear of the uncertainty permeates our way of being, and yet it cannot silence the desire we have to understand and, most of all, to live, to truly live and be free in every context of our lives. As described in the title of the New York Encounter, we yearn for the sea, and the question is, "How can we follow this yearning and not let fear have the last word in our lives?" What makes it possible to live fully and to look for happiness without being paralyzed by fear and dominated by hatred?

We have the privilege of having with us two eminent speakers who have witnessed a possibility for that in their own flesh and with their people, starting from a love, a love that is better than life. They will help us with this question. They have both lived in the Middle East and will share with us their insights, based on their life experiences. On behalf of the New York Encounter, we would like to thank Bishop Nona and Father Pizzaballa for traveling from so far to be with us today. [*applause*]

Archbishop Amel Shimoun Nona was born in November 1967 in Aqlosh, Nineveh, Iraq. He was ordained a priest in January 1991 in Bagdad. From 2000 to 2005 he studied in Rome, and from 2005 to 2010 he served as a parish priest in Aqlosh, Iraq. In January 2010 he was ordained a bishop. He served as Archbishop of the Mosul Chaldean Archdiocese from 2010 to 2014. In March 2015 he was appointed Bishop of Saint Thomas Chaldean Diocese of Australia and New Zealand. Archbishop Nona received his PhD in Theological Anthropology in 2005 from the Pontifical Lateran

University in Rome. He is the author of many books. Thank you for being with us. [*applause*]

Our next guest speaker will be Father Pierbattista Pizzaballa. Father Pizzaballa is a Franciscan Friar of the Order of the Friars Minor. He was appointed Custodian of the Holy Land for the first time in May 2004 for a period of six years, and reconfirmed by the Minister General of the Order in May 2010. He was ordained a priest in September 1990 and entered into active service of the Custody of the Holy Land in 1999. Upon completion of philosophical and theological studies, he received a Bachelor's in Theology in June 1990 from the Pontifical University Antonianum in Rome. He completed his studies of specialization at the Studium Biblicum Franciscanum in Jerusalem, obtaining his license in Biblical Theology in June 1993, and afterwards received his Master's degree from the Hebrew University of Jerusalem. He was a professor of modern Hebrew at the Franciscan faculty of Biblical and Archaeological Sciences in Jerusalem, and has done pastoral work with the Hebrew-speaking faithful for the Latin Patriarchy of Jerusalem. Welcome. [*applause*]

We will start with the Archbishop Nona. Can you tell us of your experience of faith with your community, and the contacts of conflict and persecution in your country?

Nona: Thank you, Marta. Good afternoon. First of all, I would like to thank you for inviting me to these wonderful days of the New York Encounter, and I ask you to be patient with my English, please. Faith in time of persecution. On January 16, 2010, I arrived in Mosul, the most dangerous city in Iraq at that time. I arrived as a new bishop for an old diocese that can trace the origin of its faithful community back to the end of the first century A.D. At the time of my arrival, the archdiocese had been used to having only a small number of people living there after being previously the second largest city in Iraq after Bagdad. Since the year 2003, and because of the persecution of Christians, the majority of the faithful left the city. The diocese of Mosul remained without a bishop for a period of about two years, after the kidnapping and the killing of my predecessor, Bishop Paul Faraj Rahho in 2008; and before him they killed my best friend, Father Ragheed Ganni in 2007. How could one go and live in a situation like the one that was there in Mosul in 2010? I think that the more correct question is another sort of question, which is: How can one confront persecution starting from the basis of faith? Several weeks after my arrival to Mosul, during a Mass I said to the faithful gathered in the church that our lives are worth living fully with joy and strength in every moment of it. If others want to kill us, and if I have to die an hour later, it is required for us to live life well now, rejoicing, filled with courage in the moment. The strongest weapon against terrorism is a happy life, and a truly Christian one. Islamic terrorists are well aware that the implanting of fear in others helps them stay and do what they want in the world. So, our weapons as Christians is to live without fear, show them that we love life, that we do everything to be able to live it well, and that we'll never give up this form or way of life. When they know of this, our brave choice to live life, they will not be able to do anything other than just some terrorist attacks in various forms, ultimately being the ones who lose out. I want to say that we fight them by our living of the Christian life, which counters their basic thinking and also their principles. In fact, we can still live happily, not filled with fear as happens after every terrorist attack, for example, the last terrorist attack in Paris or in San Bernardino. From my experience in Mosul I can say that we can defeat the evil incarnated in those terrorists by a solid, strong Christian life, and also the fullness of joy we use to face any evil force and show all this openly to others. Terrorists are afraid of a very happy Christian life, so let us start to become joyful Christians who are delighted in our faith in order to defeat the terrorists.

Here there is an important thing that we need to know, and that is we should not live as Christians who are in fear of terrorism, but we have to be convinced and believe that Christianity is the true way of life. There are many people who came back to Christianity because of fear. The return to faith is good, but the cause of this needs to change from fear to courage, from fear to strong conviction of the Christian faith. There is a great fear among people, I think, in the western world, maybe among you, and maybe one of the reasons for inviting me here is to know how to fight fear. I don't know. I know one thing from my experience of living in Mosul: the Christian faith is the solution. It is possible to fight fear with courage in the declaration of our faith. The declaration does not just mean the Christian example, but also the courage to talk about this model and this example, and to reveal this to everyone and everywhere. We fight fear when we believe that we are going to die someday; when? I do not know, but until I die, the question is: How do I live my life? With strength and joy because I am a Christian, if not in this place, in another; if not in Mosul, then maybe New York; if not in New York, then maybe in another place. Daesh cannot do anything when the Christians actually live as true believers. I said always: what can they do, fifty thousand people with the one billion Christians? What can they do? We have all the reason to be happy here in the Western world. You are free to live your faith, free to go to church—not like us—and you have everything to feel happy. In 2011, and specifically on Holy Thursday, we had planned for the Mass to be said during daytime in the afternoon, so that the people did not stay late in the evening and could go home safely after the Mass. The preparations were good and the people were eager for the Easter Mass with their bishop, me. I woke up in the morning and was told that there was a curfew being imposed by the army in all of Mosul, and that no one could come out in his car and even in some places not even allowed to walk. I was waiting with concern, and hoping that this curfew would be lifted before the time of the Mass, but it was not lifted. I even asked the police in the area to take me to the church to see what could be done and to establish if the Mass could go ahead even with just one or two people. And I actually went to the church accompanied by the police. The surprising thing was when I entered the church, I saw about a third of the church was filled with people, and shortly after, I saw more people coming into the church and filling it. I was amazed, because I knew they were from places and neighborhoods far away from the church. I asked them: How did you come to the church? They said: "We came by walking." There were those who walked more than an hour as a family: the father, mother and sons, daughters, and some were young women. They said when the army saw us walking, just as Christians, along on the street, they asked us: "Why do you walk when it is curfew?" They replied to them saying, "Because today is our feast." Then the army begun in some places putting them in their own army cars, and bringing them to the church. Do you know what this means to walk as a Christian family, especially women and girls, on the street when it is a prohibited day, when there is a curfew in Mosul? It means they are easy targets for anyone who wants to kill them, or for them to be abducted. When I saw the actions that these people took we began the Mass and it was very great and beautiful. If someone asks:

"How can you go to Mosul and live with fear?" I always answer them with this parable, this real example and say: "How can we not have courage when we see faith like this?" With faith and courage like this we can defeat each evil without fear.

The first Easter for me after my arrival in Mosul, I said to the faithful that we will work to have a Mass in the evening, and a late one at that, because after 2003, there were no more late and evening Masses because of fear, and because also there were curfews after 11 o'clock at night. I told them to make one Mass, and to live it with joy and as a truly spiritual moment, to face the fear with our faith, unity, and participation in our destiny. And after that, if they wish to kill us, then so be it. We actually did the Mass and to a very late hour, and it was wonderful in its spirituality and the great turnout of the faithful people, to the point of standing room only in the church, and some were even standing outside the church, too. Why was that Mass good? We challenged fear with the joy of faith and by courage and unity with each other, and the power of reason in the management of our lives, and sticking with our culture and traditions of Christianity that counter it.

I lived for four years with that terrorism in very critical conditions, so that even when I was riding in a car I would be changing the roads every time I went home or to the church. The house where I lived in was in a street closed by the army. We could not go out of it to any place without it being very difficult; but for me to get to some of the churches in the city, I needed to change my clothes and look like a normal man with no religious clothing on. O what basis do we live our lives? We have established a kind of life, based on one thing, named freedom. We fought, in the Western world especially, the fight for freedom which is really worth fighting, but we had set all of our life on this one and only basis, only freedom, freedom without truth. Due to this, from the first signs of a problem or a challenge to our freedom, we see that everything breaks down, we lose the joy and safety, we no longer feel reassured and loved. Freedom is necessary, but with the truth, with the Christian principles and values it is based on. We cannot live as a free people, without being loving, without having our Christian morals to build all aspects of our lives, such as the economy, politics, social status, and relationships in all their forms on moral and ethical values. When we deprive freedom of all of this, it remains only an idol, which means we do just what we want.

This is what a lot of people feel when confronted with terrorism. The majority are not only afraid for their life, but also for the kind of freedom that we founded our current system of life on. We need to be strong, faithful Christians and not only Sunday Mass Christians. Christians stand in front of all challenges with strength, firmness, and a lack of fear. We should not be afraid of declaring ourselves as Christians, and that our way of life is not consistent with a hope in what is produced by our current system and way of life. Christians love their haters and persecutors, but they are showing their strength and they teach them how to respect life, even if sometimes they have to resort to the use of pressure and force. To love the other does not mean you give up for what the other wants, but that you educate the nature of the other with the love that we received from our Lord Jesus. Christians do not work for the fun of the moment only, but for the moment to be filled with everything good, and not just fun. The evasiveness from responsibility in today's world, the human beings of our culture have become responsible only for themselves, and there lies the majority of our problems. Christians need to be responsible even for the wrongdoer and the villain who wants to kill us, when we do not allow him to keep doing his wickedness. Says the Lord Jesus, "If one strikes you on the right cheek, then turn to him the other also." It means halt the evildoer and show him the face that he does not know. It does not mean that we are always to be pessimistic and submissive, and to allow others to hurt us; but to even stop their evil and show them that we can hurt them. We love their humanity despite their wickedness. We need a responsible Christianity for a faith that takes responsibility for the evil and the good, and the responsibility of the whole world. Pope Francis says that there is a globalization of indifference. It is actually a malignant cancer in our body. We must be strong, not weak—witnesses to our mission and not indifferent or apathetic to what is happening around us. Maybe, you have to ask, as many they ask me, "How can we who live in the West help those persecuted Christians?" You can help the persecuted Christians when you return to preach to your community and say with courage: "We are Christians and we want a society that is Christian,"and when you declare with courage that you are Christians at every moment and in all areas of life: in the home, in relationships, at work, with friends and with people you don't know; with your social, political, and economic stances; when you do all that you can to help the persecuted Christians. There is a fear in Christianity in Western society—not from persecution, but from the new system of life that fights everything, that holds fixed values and principles. This system found an appropriate space for terrorists in order to become stronger. Christians needs to have our ethics and morals identical to our principles; our behavior shows our faith, our words translate our Christianity, thus we are filled with happiness and joy when we are being killed, as it was true of the Christian martyrs at the beginning of Christianity and is now, also in a lot of places in the world. We had a patriarch in our Chaldean Church, his name was Shimun Bar Sabbae Simon, who lived in the fourth century, martyred in the year 341 A.D. The Persian emperor at that time, King Shapur II, wanted the patriarch to deny his faith so that other Christians would leave their religion. But he refused and was sentenced to die by beheading: they cut his head. When they were taking him to the execution, along with hundreds of Christians, they had removed their clothes in the preparation for the killing. He began to sing a hymn that he composed by himself and still exists until this day and is sung in the Chaldean liturgy. I conclude my words by saying this hymn translated as, "Even so if they stripped off your outer clothes, do not take off your inner clothes, dear baptized faithful, for if you are dressed with this invisible weapon, then not even the waves of many temptations could defeat you." Thank you. [*applause*]

Zaknoun: We will now watch a short video that will illustrate a bit of what we heard from Bishop Nona. It's a piece of an interview with a family of Christian Iraqi refugees in Erbil. I think the interview and the answer of the mother and the interview speaks for itself, it needs no explanation.

[VIDEO]

Zaknoun: After what we've heard from Archbishop Nona and the short video, we would like also to ask Father Pizzaballa about his experience of faith in a slightly different context, which is the context of the Holy Land. We would like to hear about your experience of faith within the diversity of the context of the Holy Land and what it implies for your relationship with the other and whomever is different from us.

Pizzaballa: Thank you. To talk about the challenges of faith in this context, first of all you have to look at this context, which is very problematic right now. We have to be very clear and transparent on this. First of all, what we are seeing in the Middle East is not just one of the periodical crisis we see continuously in the Middle East in the Holy Land, or in the whole Middle East. I think we are at a sort of an epic change, dramatic change; the Middle East won't be as it was in the past century, it will be something new, different, and we don't know how it will be. And one of the purposes of this war is to define who will rule, who will be the main power of the Middle East, especially what is going on in Syria. Syria and Iraq, as we heard, is a proxy war where many elements are present. Everyone knows about the Sunnis and Shias. Behind the Sunnis is Saudi Arabia, behind the Shia is Iran; and then the Western countries on one side, Russia and China on the other side, fighting for power and a redefinition of the new Middle East. All these things everyone can find in the news, in all the different analyses about what is going on in the Middle East. And there is, of course, religious fundamentalism growing, a fact whether we like or not, especially in the Islamic world, that affects the life of all. It's not just against the Christians, as we have said, it's a war among themselves, inside the Islamic world, but affects also the other minorities. We've heard in the Middle East there are Druze, Yazidis, Kurds, and many other minorities of different groups. It's a reality that all these minorities are targeted by ISIS and other affiliated groups, and even by other Muslims who don't accept their way life.

I don't want to appear cynical, but sooner or later this war will finish and our concern is not just about the war, but what will be after the war. These wars are not just destroying the infrastructures and the countries, they are destroying relations among the different communities, especially Christians, Muslims, and other minorities. It will be very difficult to rebuild the trust, the mutual trust among the different communities, and this is the challenge, because we Christians will remain in Middle East, we won't leave Middle East. Not at all. We remain in Middle East in a small number, but we remain there, we won't leave. And the Muslims also will remain there. Our future is exactly where we were in the past: together.

Like it or not, we have to build our future together. To rebuild trust that has been wounded, deeply wounded by this war, will be very difficult. I don't know if it is possible to have dialogue among religions. I'm skeptical, but I believe in dialogue among believers of the different religions, starting from the experience of faith. And faith cannot be discussed, but can be shared. In any case, in this big sea of evil there are questions that the politicians have to answer, but I'm not a politician. I cannot give answers. I cannot change. I have not the power to change the politics and to resolve all the questions.

What all this says to me as a person, and first of all as a Christian believer, as a Franciscan: all this sea, just to use the title, this sea of evil that we are seeing, not just in the Middle East that is scaring us, we are afraid from a human point of view what is going on, we don't know if tomorrow we will be alive or not, especially in some parts of Syria they will take you, kidnap you; we have from Bishop Nona some examples. What does it say to me as person? I have to say that we cannot destroy all the evil. The purpose of a Christian faith, our faith, we as Christians, we don't want the world to be rid of evil: this is the program of the Antichrist, not our program. If we want the world to get rid of evil, we have to deprive men of the freedom to commit evil; and the freedom, the freedom that Carrón talked about, is the consequence of the Christian faith, at least from the Christian point of view. This provokes us as Christians, as believers, in our faith.

What is faith? I want to give some examples. All of the Christian community reacted in front of the evil that is going on there. We are in Syria now, North Syria, three villages: Qunaya, Yacoubieh, and Jdeideh, three small villages, Christian villages, Catholic and Orthodox: only the Catholic priest remains there, and these villages are under the control of Jabhat-al-Nusra and Al-Qaeda. Al Qaeda is a moderate movement in comparison to Daesh,ISIS; it is moderate. [*laughter*] Under ISIS, if you are Christian you cannot remain, but under Al-Nusra you have a lot of restrictions; leaving is better, but you can remain under certain conditions. The conditions are: no Christian symbols, no crosses, no statues, no icons, no wine—alcohol as you know is forbidden; you have to remove all the Christian symbols, not just from outside these villages but also from inside the houses, even from inside the churches: nothing can remain, we have to remove everything. When they entered into power they came to destroy all these symbols.

The villages are very poor villages; farmers, in the country, and these few Christians that remain, they didn't allow the fighters of Jabhat-al-Nusra to touch their symbols. If you want us to remove them, we remove them, but you don't touch them, we will do it; and they respectfully concealed all the symbols. They celebrated a kind of funeral. You know, the Christians in the Middle East used to have the symbol of the cross, or Saint George, or Saint Michael, on the door of the entrance. They covered these with plaster, but no one else can touch the symbols, the symbols of our faith. Wine, as I said, is forbidden. If they find you with wine, you are immediately arrested, brought to the Islamic Court. But these simple Christians, simple in a good sense, they didn't study theology and they hide wine, each family, one week per family they hide the wine because they want the Eucharist, they cannot live without the Eucharist. In front of all this problematic situation, their answer was: I remain, I don't give up, I don't renounce, I want to remain attached.

I now want to read a testimony of a Franciscan that you know very well: Father Ibrahim, who was sent to Aleppo a little more than a year ago. Maybe someone of you heard, because after he sent us his testimony, he distributed it to all the others. I quote: "With this message there is in us the certainty that God is present even now, even here in the rubble of Aleppo, that the gates of hell shall not prevail and that the Lord will always bring forth more goodness for those who love Him, even out of this evil. We continue to encourage our people to hope against all hope, carrying with courage the daily cross. In our assiduous prayer we found the energy to continue to see with the eye of the heart that there is something beautiful and bright that awaits the Church of East, after this storm. The wait is not in vain, a wait for a new period for the witness and the expansion of the kingdom of God." Father Ibrahim brought this after his church was hit by a bomb a few months ago, when the church was packed with Christians praying the rosary before Mass. Such a reaction should not be taken for granted. Father Dhiya Aziz is a Franciscan from Iraq, the parish priest in the church of Yacoubieh. He has been kidnapped twice in Syria. The first time he was kidnapped, a few months ago in July, from a group affiliated to Jabhat Al-Nusra, Jaish al-Fatah, and he was not liberated; he managed to escape thanks to a Muslim sheik who helped him escape from there. He saw, this sheik, that there is something strange in the house that was abandoned because of the bombs. He saw new life, so he wanted to see if there is someone that needs help. He discovered it was a group of Jihadists who had a priest. During the night he helped him to escape. He distracted some of the guards, then helped him to escape. In a very funny way, through the window like in a movie, with blankets and so on, and then with a motorcycle he carried him for two hours, far from the prison where he was, he gave him money and the name of a family where he could go to be helped. And this is also a reaction that should not be taken for granted.

Father Dhiya was kidnapped a second time, just before Christmas, by another group. After the first kidnapping I said to him: "You have every right to leave, if you want," and he was upset with me. He said: "I have to go back to my parish, to my people, I cannot leave them." And this is also not a reaction to take for granted. Now the second time, one of the conditions for his liberation was that he leave Syria. His parish would be without a priest and we would have to decide whether to send another priest or not. There remained just eighty persons in this parish, eighty in Yakoubieh, about a hundred in Qunaya, about seventy to eighty in Jdeideh. Just one priest remained there, one Franciscan priest. Now we had to decide what to do. To send another one would mean another likely kidnapping, or even a killing as happened to Father François Murad and some others. I consulted all the friars: What do you think? What do I have to do? I sent an e-mail to all the friars, about three hundred, and they answered: even if there will be less than eighty, even if there are only two who remain, we have to go. We cannot leave them, it is our duty, it is our mission, we have to be present there, and even if we will be killed—in any case, we have to go. This is the reason for which we are here. Next week, then, a new priest from Jordan will go there. He's too young in my opinion, but anyway. All these examples are not just to praise our priest, because many others are doing the same; I am simply saying that in all of this evil there is a provocation, and the answer can be the refusal, no hope, nothing to do, it's better to leave, to escape or to fight this. Or it can be the other answer, the answer that we see many Christians give.

Just few examples. We can give the answer that only the faith can give. From a human point of view you see just desolation, destruction, the end of the world that we were part of. The faith is able to see, like Father Ibrahim said, something more that goes beyond what you see. The prophet Isaiah talks about the earthly Jerusalem: a wonderful city full of peace and joy; but what was in front of his human eyes was desolation. Jerusalem was destroyed, was not a beautiful city. He was able to see something different because his eyes were full of hope and faith that became the certainty.

In front of all this evil we have to remain human, and to remain human means to remain Christian. For us, the Christian faith is the fullness of our humanity. And I saw a lot of evil, as did Bishop Nona—destruction and hatred—but I see also wonderful examples of life, wonderful examples of people who are ready to give their life but not to abandon their people, not to abandon their faith, their Jesus, who is the answer that, in their full freedom, the freedom that Father Carrón talked about today, they were able to give. This says to me that I don't know how the Middle East will be in the future. I have no idea. No one knows. But one thing I know: through the example of the priests, friars, people, simple people, that we will be part of this future, the Christian faith will remain, and it will be the light that will enlighten the Middle East and the Holy Land, where the situation is different but also complicated. s I don't know what, when, and who, but I know we will be there. Thank you. [*applause*]

Zaknoun: Thank you very much, Father Pizzaballa. We're just gonna ask a couple of questions to our speakers, just to expand on a couple of aspects. First, Archbishop Nona, you mentioned helping our Christian brothers in the Middle East. Can you expand on this? How do you think we are called to be as Christians in our context? Because I think this is the greatest challenge now for us.

Nona: I think it's very easy: to be Christians. To live your faith, because you have here everything to live your faith in a very easy way. You can go to church every Sunday without fear, for example; you can live in your house with other people without fear. I think it's very easy to live our Christian life and our faith here, and very important to be happy, because there is no reason to not be happy. There are many difficulties in our lives in the

Western world, yes, but so what? Always we have difficulties in our lives, but it's very important that we are free to live our faith, it's a grace from our God to have this freedom to live your faith, not like other people. I remember when I was in Mosul, going to the church always was, in a sense, going to die, because you didn't know when you go if you'll come back to your house. Always. But even with that situation, every Sunday the church was full of Christians, and they were happy. The most important thing that you can do here, in the Western world, is to be happy in your life, because you have all the reasons to be happy, the most important reason being that you have the faith, the Christian faith, and I think there's nothing else to do or say.

Zaknoun: Thank you. One more question to Father Pizzaballa: you talked about the possibility not only that Christianity remains, but that there is a possibility of living with other people. There is an openness that is desirable and attractive in what you're saying to us. Often, in our context, even within not so confrontational situations, we withdraw, because we feel that the other is something distant. In the North American or European context, we don't have the engagement that you happen to have in the Middle East, even with these difficulties. What can you say to us, here in North America, how can you help us with that?

Pizzaballa: I'm not a prophet, nor a son of prophets. It is true that in the Holy Land, but also in all the Middle East, the relationships in the community are very close, the communities are very close to one another and their lives are very well connected. All the different communities have to deal one with another. Muslims with Jews, Jews with Christians, and Christians with all the others and so on. Quite often we also have problems, and because of that we have to deal continuously with one another. This is problematic, of course, but also a wonderful opportunity of encounter, challenging also your faith. Your faith, your culture, your relations with the other, because you are always provoked—positively provoked in your faith, in your Christianity. Why are you doing this, why are you Christians doing this, we are so different, why you are so different?—all these questions come and we have to answer why Jesus is a wonderful person, why we have to resurrect, for instance: all these questions about faith that help you think about your faith. This sometimes is a source of problems, as I've said, but became also a very positive challenge in our relations. Here, the different communities remains all in this way distinct. In the Middle East, though, we have continuous relations among us, while here the challenge is different, is integration, because the communities are integrating in the same society but we have the impression that there are no relations. We are very isolated one from the another. Fear is always wrong. You can, from a certain point of view, understand the fear of the other; but our experience is that the other can sometimes be painful, can wound you, but also enrich you, make you richer. It helps you to broaden your horizons and see reality always in a different way. I don't have lessons to give, but I think that dialogue, positive dialogue, is important when you share not the faith, but the experience of faith, and that it's possible also here and it has to be done, otherwise you remain just a small island, and this is very risky.

Zaknoun: I think you would agree with me that what we heard today is a powerful testimony, a testimony of the love that makes life possible and that makes giving one's life possible, it makes hope possible. We heard today something that will allow us to leave the harbor: a lived faith, and the certainty of an answer for our yearning. This testimony automatically becomes an invitation to us, an invitation to question and challenge how we face our circumstances that may be less tragic than in the Middle East, yet nevertheless dramatic; an invitation not to stop at the level of opinions and analyses, but to go deeper to the origin of the question. Thank you, Father Pizzaballa and Archbishop Nona, for sharing your lives with us and challenging us. We leave this encounter today with a hypothesis to verify. Let us discover if there is a love in our lives that makes life worth living, and that can challenge every circumstance; something that is given to us so that we can face things without fear and with lots of expectation. Thank you.

longing for the Sea
and yet
not afraid

EXIT

Longing for You and With You Not Afraid

Concluding remarks with ***Maurizio Maniscalco****, President of New York Encounter, and* ***John Waters****, author*

Introduction

"If the most convincing evidence today seems to be what is in fashion, where can people find themselves again? Where can they find their own original identity? The answer that I am about to give not only fits the current situation, but it's a rule, a universal law (since the beginning until the end of human existence): people regain themselves in a living encounter, that is, by means of bumping into a presence that stirs an attraction and provokes them to recognize that their 'heart'— with the needs of which it is made —does exist! The 'I' again finds itself in an encounter with a presence that carries this statement: 'What your heart is made for does exist! You see in me, for example, that it exists.' In fact, paradoxically, the originality of the self emerges when we realize we have in us something that is in everybody (and, by the way, this is what really puts us in relationship with others and makes us no longer feel like strangers). People rediscover their original identity by encountering a presence that gives rise to an attraction, reawakens the heart, and causes a commotion full of reasonableness, because it matches the needs of life according to all of its dimensions, from birth to death. People regain themselves when a presence, which corresponds to the needy nature of existence, finds its way into their life—only in this way may the person no longer be lonely. Usually, in daily life, people live in a solitude from which they try to escape by means of imagination and discourse. However, this presence which corresponds to life is the opposite of imagination. The encounter allowing the self to rediscover itself is not a 'cultural' meeting, but a living encounter; it is not a speech, but a living 'fact'—which, of course, may emerge even by hearing someone speak;

Sunday, January 17, 2015

however, it is always a matter of a relationship with something living, not an ideology or a discourse disconnected from the force of life." (Msgr. Luigi Giussani, excerpt from a talk given to university students in Italy in August 1987)

What is the final word on man's desire? Is there an attraction capable of overcoming our fears and drawing us out to the open waters that our hearts yearn for?

Maniscalco: John, welcome back to the Encounter. You've been here before.

Waters: Thank you very much. It's nice to be here.

Maniscalco: Listen. As we were saying before, just between you and me, we can't really wrap it all up and say, Okay, here's the finished product of whatever this thing was.

Waters: You know, I was just thinking that really, we need to come back in a week or ten days, and then give a kind of preliminary gestation of what we've experienced. Also, for me, there was kind of a curve-ball thrown in there at the last Encounter, with Father Pizzaballa and Archbishop Nona, because I've been trying to synthesize—that's the word you used—and obviously, coming from a personal perspective, coming here from Ireland and coming to New York and all that, and seeing this thing going on and equating these things with New York outside, in my heart and in my life; and then, it's not that I've forgotten, but these guys remind me that out there, there are people with seriously real problems. That maybe for a moment, make my perception of my own problems, or the problems of my society, or the problems of our culture kind of, quite, high class, and that kind of threw me. But I think I can get my head around that in a few days. I know there is a context in this because, you know when you see those two guys talking, they're two men talking, it's not like a TV discussion. And I hope this isn't either. But they're two men talking. It's for real. They're two hearts engaging with their life and with their experience and sharing it, not making political points, not making ideological points, it's not trying to provide an analysis, and I hope we're not going to do that either.

So, that's the first thing I kind of need to factor in there. The thing that stands out for me immediately, as the kind of single event of this weekend, was the opening event, Christopher Wiman. I thought, there's something completely emblematic of the times about this guy and his work. I hadn't heard of him before, I hadn't come across him; shame on me.

Maniscalco: Okay, now you have to explain what you mean by that.

Waters: Well, I've been picking up some of his books and reading them the last few days. What he was talking about is faith. In this moment, in this place, here we are in New York in the center of the world, the center of my world, the world, the Western world, whatever you call it, Western Civilization, and we know that we'll come back and it's the problem of believing, the problem of skepticism, the problem of what I will kind of controversially call "the implausibility of Christianity in culture" that we have to deal with every day. When you get up and you go and face the world, and the din of the street, and the racket of the street, and the blur of that. Most of the time you're carrying doubt more than faith. If you want to speak the language of the world and of the street, you're speaking doubt in yourself, in your own heart. I thought that was really interesting. Here you have a poet, and poets are the only people that can get this; that the problem of faith is not necessarily skepticism as such, the problem is language. Because we all attach our understandings of reality to words, we put them up in front of us as explanations for who we are and what we are, and we meet the explanation of others first in their words. And poets understand that this is actually contingent, it's provisioned. Words are—as Giussani said, we use the least inadequate words. So, words are not the thing. And yet, we have to use words. There is a poem, which I hope to read before we finish, a section of a poem by an Irish poet who I've been trying to sell to the world for the last, I don't know, many years—Patrick Kavanagh.

Maniscalco: You get commissions? [*laughter*]

Waters: If Giussani had come across Kavanagh, he would have said, "We don't need Leopardi and those guys, [*laughter*] it's all here."

Maniscalco: I'm not the official defender of orthodoxy here, but be careful. I'm Italian, amongst other things, so leave Leopardi alone, okay? [*laughter*]

Waters: I like Leopardi, too, but Patrick Kavanagh was really a mystic in Ireland in the '50s, he died quite young. He died in his early sixties, and as you and I know, that's very young. But he had a brother called Peter, who was twelve years younger, who wanted to be a poet himself. But he didn't become a poet because Patrick told him you can only have one poet in any family.

Maniscalco: Yeah, somebody gotta work.

Waters: So Peter decided, Well, if that is the case...and he worked here in New York. Patrick was completely ignorant, particularly of poetry; he was a genius, a great poet, great mystic, but he knew nothing about poetry. So Peter came to New York to learn about poetry, and he became a professor of poetry here in New York. He called himself Patrick's sacred-keeper, and he said that poetry is not literature, it's theology. I became friendly with Peter, he lived into his nineties. And the most beautiful definition of a poem I ever heard—because they used to talk about the flash of the other coming in—I said, Where do the words come into this? What are the words? And he said, Ah. He said in a poem the words are the least important part. In a poem, the words burn up in a tremendous thread of something unusual.

And that's what Wiman really understands. That he's dealing with words, but he's actually talking about something beyond. And that's the only way we can get out of the block that culture is imposing on our belief, the skepticism that it's imposing on us. Because we import all these words, and we try to order them in our heads, and order them around us so that we understand the world in a verbal way. And we need to do that. But it's also a huge problem. Wiman understands that. I thought it was incredible; but also he was incredible at the level of the doubter, that he belonged more with doubters. Because I'm a doubter. That's probably more controversial than the Leopardi quote. But I'm not a doubter, I don't say, this didn't happen, that didn't happen; I'm not that kind of doubter. I'm somebody who's full of doubt every day, and at the same time, is convinced in another way, by the evidence of my own existence.

Maniscalco: Hold on a second. We focused on fear, in many ways. Now you're bringing up doubt. Is it the same thing? Is it different?

Waters: Yeah, it is. And I want to read to you, if I can, if I can find the piece, this paragraph I found in this amazing book, *My Bright Abyss: Meditation of a Modern Believer*, by Christian Wiman. He's describing his sickness, what happened as a result of sickness.

"Last night my wife and I finally fell asleep after talking and crying about our life together and the life of our children—the splendor of some moments, so many moments, the gift we have been given; and then the misery of my sickness and the way it is crushing us, the terror the two of us feel of what will happen if (I won't write 'when,' but we are now always thinking it) I die.

I wake in the night with a terror that is purer, further than my own. My suffering is the key but not the content, and for an hour I am silvered with an icy, infinite distance, an abyss of pure meaninglessness of which I am merely some small and dreadfully sentient particle. I am not dreaming. I've never been more awfully awake. A spot of time, and what the spot shows, this time, is nothingness, suffering without meaning."

This is fear becoming doubt, doubt becoming fear. Where I grew up in Ireland, you're not allowed to express doubts. I mean Doubting Thomas was a villain; he was a bad guy. He has the mustache, like all those guys in the movies. [*laughter*] He was up there with Judas. Judas was slightly worse, but not a lot. I always had a sneaking regard for Doubting Thomas, because I thought, Well, he just asked for some evidence–is that so wrong? I kind of think if I'd been there I'd be doing the same thing. I don't mean that in any blasphemous way, but I just think that that's a good thing. Without Doubting Thomas, we wouldn't know as certainly as we do about these things; we know more certainly what happened because of Thomas. So I think that Thomas is, like, the patron saint of the modern era because we're all doubters, we're all skeptics. How could you be otherwise in a world that doesn't acknowledge these things?

Maniscalco: True. Let me interrupt you, though. You come over here—you, myself, thousands of people who have been with us over this weekend, and, I guess, inside us doubt and fear do exist. Yet, you look around and you see gladness. How does that work?

Waters: Oh, it's amazing, because you might think, and the world out there would think, that this is a kind of a group huddle of mutual reassurance. But that's not what it's like. I mean, I think of New York as the center of the world. It's a place that is mythical. It's built by my ancestors, your ancestors and, we don't know how they did it. It's like I look at all those buildings, those tall buildings, and I kind of think they're like blunted steeples on the one hand, but they're also kind of stunted towers of Babel. Somewhere in between is that kind of desire for the infinite and still a kind of desire to make man the center of the world. And this is the place where, if you can sort of live it here, you can live it anywhere. This is a great place, this is the Encounter, this is where the test is, this is kind of Cape Canaveral, or whatever you call it.

This is the first year I've come to the Encounter that I actually had some time to do something other than come from the airport, talk, and then go back again. Myself, me and my wife, we went off, we were vagabonding around Manhattan on Friday all day, and giving thanks for everything. Particularly for climate change, because it was such a beautiful day. [*laughter*]

Maniscalco: It's beautiful now because it's snowing.

Waters: I know you prefer it the way it was. You're a traditionalist. [*laughter*]

I came here with the mentality I feel most of the time, and I would call it—a kind of inversion—it's almost like when you're looking in the wrong end of the telescope you see things upside down. That's the way it is most of the time in the world. Because you think that faith, religion, all these, whatever word you want to use, is a small part of reality. And that the reality, the big thing, is something else, it's the secular world, it's the kind of irreligious world. And here in this building, in the last three days, I kind of was able to turn it upside down again, to look into the right side of the telescope again. Not as they say, a kind of a group reassurance, but because of the way things were being talked about, and looking into the eyes of people like Christian Wiman, and Father Pizzaballa, and all these people who hold this certainty, and can articulate it so beautifully. That gives me affirmation for my heart, because the big problem in the modern world, I think, is that we all have this thing going on in our heart, all the questions. But the din of the outside world, it drowns it out for us, even we can't hear it. Even this short distance, we can't hear what's going on in our heart. It's really important that we get this kind of circuitry going with other hearts, which is what happens here. And you think, Ah, no, no, I see things now again, I'm reminded. That's what I think Christian was saying about the faith; it's really keeping true to the moments of faith in your own life. That's very often the best you can do.

Going back, I remember when I believed very strongly, I remember a moment when I was certain. because a lot of the time I have to—Giussani's really beautifully helpful in this, because Giussani's almost like a mathematician; he gives you all the evidences, all the access to the evidences, the method to put the evidences together. It's almost like an algebraic equation. There's my desire, there is the witness, there is the correspondence that I feel. The unanswered questions that I feel, the very fact that I'm here, is something that I'm liable to forget back in Ireland.

People say to me, C'mon. My colleagues, my former colleagues, I'm no longer a journalist, I gave it up; not all unrelated to this. Sometimes my colleague says, C'mon, you're an intelligent guy, how can you really believe the Son of God came here 2,000 years ago and died on the cross? I say, Yeah, and thanks to Giussani I have the answer. I say, Yeah, it is a bit improbable, I guess, but it's not nearly as improbable as the fact that I came, myself, that I'm here now. I'm here in this world, I'm here right now, looking out of this world, asking, What the hell is going on?

Maniscalco: So, sticking to that—

Waters: This is why it's so important to be here and to see something that engages with the world totally, not in a religious way, in the way that we kind of have been told that small part of the world is religious.

Maniscalco: But what if this is a dream? And then tomorrow we go back to our daily life, and doubt and fear?

Waters: But it wears off, and that's no good. We have to hold onto it when we go back. It's a really hard thing to do. But the memory of it, of all this, is going to help, provided you keep going. You remember how you saw the world for these days. You remember how other people looked at you and took for granted that the things that are dear to you are dear to them and are true and real. I think that's what we have to work on. That's the point of the community of faith. We can't do it all alone, we will lose it if we try to do it all on our own.

Maniscalco: I've never been much of a believer, and to make a long story short, I owe it to Father Giussani. And one of the first things that I learned from Father Giussani was this strange definition of faith. It was strange for me, the recognition of a Presence. Which is not exactly what my answer would have been to a question like, What is faith? I was a teenager, I had no idea. Well, if I think about this, and I try to connect to your point about memory that you just now brought up, tomorrow the experience of faith would be the memory of something that we have seen and touched and experienced. Something present. Not a feeling or... [*gestures*]

Waters: I'm thinking of Tom Jones and that talk he gave. It resonates with previous things I've heard from Buzz Aldrin, John Glenn, and Neil Armstrong. There's a very strange kind of paradox the way the world sees these guys as adventurers, as opposed to the way they see themselves and the way they see the world. I've noticed this again and again. We in the modern secular world will watch this stuff on TV, and something about it tells us, Hey, we're in charge, man is moving through the stratosphere. We're taking over everything. Who is God? He's nothing, it's obvious we're in charge. This happened to me one night, actually, when I was giving a talk about Patrick Kavanagh and talking about the mysticism of Patrick Kavanagh, and at the end there were some questions, and this guy stood up and said, Hey, c'mon, we're sick and tired of listening to all this stuff. I came here for a talk about Patrick Kavanagh. I didn't want a lecture on Catholicism. And he says, Don't you realize that man has been to the moon? [*laughter*] Wow, that's a hard one. Thanks to Giussani, I had the answer. It was like, my father would have called this a smart answer, by which in Ireland we mean a smart aleck. So it popped out, Have *you* been to the moon? And it turned out that he hadn't, luckily. [*laughter*]

I said, How has it changed your life? How has it changed your heart, that Neil Armstrong went to the moon, and walked on the moon? How has it changed your heart? Because when Neil Armstrong came back, he had to go to bed and sleep, and then he got up in the morning, and he looked in the bathroom mirror—I presume—and he still saw the same face, and he had the same question: Who is Neil Armstrong, and why? So nothing is changed but the progress. There is this thing about people like Tom Jones. You can see their faith is really strong, and yet down here we take their adventuring as evidence for our complacency and skepticism and our sense of hubris. I also read an interesting contradiction, that the guys that actually do the work and take the risks are not like that. I met Tom Jones, he was in the same hotel as me, we came out of our bedrooms this morning, and there he was, waiting for the elevator. Astronauts have to use elevators. [*laughter*] Who knew that?

So, I kind of asked him on the way down, I asked him a few questions. I asked him about the fear thing, Were you never afraid up there? He said, I was afraid that we hadn't prepared properly. I thought that was kind of a bland answer. But I said, When you were up there, did you ever think, this is a crazy thing to be doing? And he said, No, it's what I always wanted, it's what I always longed for, why would I be afraid? That's the right answer.

Maniscalco: That's the key.

Waters: That's the right answer, isn't it? I also told him my Tom Jones joke. I said, Tom Jones, do you know there's another Tom Jones? Do people in America know who Tom Jones really is?

Maniscalco: The real one, you mean?

Waters: Yeah! I mean, I was kinda gonna say to Tom, ya know, I would call myself Thomas if I was you. [*laughter*] Because it's like being called Johnny Cash or something. So I says, Ya know, I tried telling my Tom Jones joke, which I told you. This guy goes to the doctor, right? And he says, Doctor, doctor, I don't know what's wrong with me. I keep singing "The Green Green Grass of Home." By the way, if you don't get the joke, it's because you're Americans. [*laughter*] This joke was actually voted the best joke ever by the readers of the *Daily Telegraph* in London.

Maniscalco: Yeah, but that's a different world.

Waters: My wife here thinks it's the worse joke she's ever heard, but she doesn't read the *Daily Telegraph*. So, "Doctor, doctor, what's wrong with me? I keep singing 'The Green Green Grass of Home.'" And he says, "Ah, yeah, that's Tom Jones Syndrome." And he says, "Oh, is that common?" "Well, it's not unusual." [*laughter*] The other Tom said to me, "I didn't see that coming."

Isn't it an amazing paradox, though, that we take some kind of sustenance for our skepticism, our hubris, and they just feel the wonder and astonishment of looking at God's universe from up there? We should really think about this stuff. Because we're in our small, centrally-heated rooms—Pope Benedict talked about the bunker that man built for himself so that he can shut out the mystery. We're here watching him on TV and thinking, There ya go, man has been to the moon. And the astronauts are thinking, *God is.*

Maniscalco: Well, which is like being in front of the sea and having to make up your mind and decide, Shall I sail or shall I stay? Which is, I believe, a daily challenge. It's not something that you decide once in a lifetime and that's about it. You take the boat, the boat is safe in the harbor, for sure, but it's not meant to stay there. I'm not meant to stay there. But what allows me to take that step?

Waters: Faith. Faith that you can find, that's what you have to construct. That's the antidote to fear: faith. To know. Again, I loved, if I can remember correctly what Christian said on Friday night that faith is a... I can't remember exactly how he put it, but faith is to risk believing, to risk thinking it will be okay. To risk thinking everything will be okay. What a risk that would be. You know, skepticism is really a crippling thing. It brings fear along with it.

Let me tell you a story I've told before, but it just shows again how Giussani helped me in ways. When my daughter was growing up—she's now twenty—she's in Dublin and always had amazing insights into this whole thing about God, and she'd no difficulty in comprehending the place of God in her life and all that. But when she got to be thirteen, I remember one day, very clearly, when she was thirteen, we were out in Spain, and we were with my two nephews and they were kind of older and more typical young Irish Catholics, which means they believe in absolutely nothing. So, they were kind of laying it on thick, and I wasn't really getting involved. But that night, she tapped on my bedroom door, and she said, Dad, I'm terrified. I'm terrified that there's nothing. That's a really heavy moment. You know it's going to come, but you never prepare. And it comes suddenly, and you know if you utter a platitude, it's over. If you say, "There, there, it'll be okay," forget it—finished. Luckily, I had encountered Giussani and I'd read *The Religious Sense*, and I remembered—to me the most important, is page 100 of *The Religious Sense*, that paragraph about imagining that you've just been born. Imagine that you're coming out of your mother's womb at this moment. I said to Róisín, "Okay, go back to the day you were born." I didn't quite give her the Giussani version, because I kind of thought that was a bit glib for me to come out with, so I said, "Imagine, go back to the day you'd been born. And don't stop there, go back another nine months to the day"—that was the tenth of March, 1996. "Go back nine months more, let's say to the tenth of June, 1995, that's the day you were conceived, say. But don't stop there, go back one more day, before you were conceived. Before you were anything, before you could even be thought about by anybody. And you can bring with you all"—as Giussani says—"bring everything you've learned, all your experience, all your language, all your emotions, everything you have up to that moment. And I want to ask you a question. What, in that moment, do you think is possible? Is Spain possible? Is the Mediterranean possible? Am I possible? Are you possible? Is anything possible? I should know, nothing's possible—in that moment nothing's possible." So I said, "Why then, you're here, in the midst of everything, in Spain, the Mediterranean is there, I'm here, you're here, you have your life, everything is here. And you're thinking about nothingness. You're afraid of nothing. You're afraid of the abyss. You're afraid of something somebody has told you is gonna happen to you. Why? I mean, what kind of reason is it to be in the midst of everything and be thinking of nothing?" That's where the fear comes from. As Giussani says, the fear of losing what we have cripples us and stops our living in it. I said, That's not reasonable. I'm so grateful to Giussani for that alone, if nothing else, I would be ahead with Giussani. Because Róisín's studying theology at Trinity College; so far, she's kind of on the road. She still understands, in her own way, what this is about.

Fear. Fear is such a waste of time. I'm an alcoholic. I haven't had a drink for twenty-five years, through the grace of God. Alcoholism is a symptom, a disease of modernity. A lot of these additions are fundamentally that, because they're based on fear. The fear of having taken over from God. Having usurped the role of God, having banished God. And if you banish God you have to take his place on the throne. But the problem with being on the throne, on God's throne, is you have all the responsibilities in your own life, but none of the power. And you're screwed. That's kind of what I had to learn to stop drinking. I had to actually allow God back in, to do the stuff that he used to do. So I resigned as CEO of John Waters, Inc. [*laughter*] And I invited God back from retirement, and he took over. And things have been going swimmingly ever since, as you can see. [*applause*]

Maniscalco: Well, you told this story, and I was tempted to tell a story myself. But I'm not sure how I'm gonna tell the story. I know for a fact that every time I didn't stop at the level of fear, every time I took that step, I went beyond the threshold of what would have been under my control, it's always been because of an Other. But somebody real, not...well, I'll tell you the story as briefly as I can. I'm sixty-one years old, and I belong to a European generation, we were all ideologically Marxist, even though we didn't know what that meant. It was what it was supposed to be. Among other things, I was a fierce enemy of Communion and Liberation as a teenager. At some point, curiosity and desire, and sadness, I would say, compelled me to try to take a step. And since I've always been fairly wild, I decided that I wanted to go to Milan to see Father Giussani, okay? So I'm gonna take the "boat," I'm going to go to Milan. You know, for a kid born and raised in a small beach town like Pizarro, forty-plus years ago, that was a big step. And I went. I went because of a need. I needed a father. Maybe I did not understand what a father is, but I understood that I needed a father. Somebody who could take me by the hand and help me understand my heart and live my life. I didn't know where to look, but at least I was curious enough to take the train, not the boat, and go to Milan. You don't go to Milan by boat. There was the promise, the desire.

After ten days in Milan, I wanted to go back. I was ready to bring my boat back to the harbor. Because at least I knew my harbor. Instead, I was in unknown territory and surrounded by unfamiliar faces and at time hostile feelings. But then something happened. Because what makes a difference is something that happens and that you are forced to acknowledge. Not something that you make happen. I didn't make happen a damn thing. I was sitting in a classroom, hiding behind a newspaper, and I was thinking about going back home, for real, meaning my hometown, when a throng of people storms into the room. The next thing I remember, there's an old man—he was only fifty-two by then but looked old to me, because I was young—sitting next to me, and he goes, "What are you doing here all by yourself?" It was my first close encounter with Father Giussani. I have a vague recollection of how that conversation went. But it's like saying, I'm on this boat, I don't know where to go, somebody's taken the helm, somebody who mysteriously cares for me, loves me for what I am. Doesn't measure me according to my pettiness, or weaknesses. Embraces me, and tells me, Be not afraid. The promise becomes real for me. It's always happened like that, even here, this weekend. The promise becomes real in the flesh. I wouldn't know how else to put it. This is way bigger, this is way more beautiful, this is way more mine, than anything I could possibly create. If you'll allow me, then, I'll leave you the final six minutes and then I gotta thank everybody.

I want to read this thing from Father Giussani. A miracle, because for me, this is a miracle.

A miracle is a human reality lived out daily without emphasis on the exceptional. Without any need for exceptions. Without any particularly good fortune. It is the reality of eating, drinking, waking, and sleeping, invested by the awareness of a Presence that exists in hands touching, in faces which can be seen, in a pardon which can be given, in money to be shared, in a burden to bear, in a task to be accepted.

What do you think?

Waters: The thing about Giussani, the first thing I started to notice about him was, he didn't let anything go. He insisted that everything was significant. Everything. And the world had told me something different, even though I had an experience that somehow confirmed what he was saying. I still was convinced that these were kind of coincidences or something. Giussani kept saying things like, *Follow reality*. I didn't know what that meant at first, but only gradually. So he's saying to me that the things that happened to me today are significant. They're not incidental, they're not accidental. The thing again about the opening Friday night, that passage about the Chopin piece. I mean, that's incredible. To describe so beautifully, something that everybody might miss. To capture, and to admit that he missed it himself as well.

Maniscalco: As the actress, the reader, said after the presentation Friday evening, I've never read anything like this.

Waters: Yeah. Who is this guy? How did he see though all this stuff? So many of the things that Giussani has said, you kind of have thought yourself, but maybe you've dismissed them. And then he puts it all together. I really think, though, the challenge for us now in the next period, is to... Christian said about speaking to non-believers, that's kind of where he belongs. As a former journalist, I kind of used to get into wars with non-believers, atheists. I used to be an atheist myself, but I still used to get into wars, and they used to get into wars with me. I kind of wish I could get out of that. That's partly why I'm not writing anymore. I realized I got into a certain rush of defending things; that's the wrong way. Albacete used to have a beautiful way, I don't know how he did it. He used to be able to say things and not fall out with anybody. Everybody loved him because of the way he was, not because they agreed with him. He'd write in the *New York Times*, and he was really going across enemy lines, as it were, and he didn't behave like that.

I think we need to find a way to create a language that will jump the gate. And that's what I really picked up from Christian on Friday night. A great poet, again, I didn't think that we'd see another Kavanagh at this stage. Fifty years later, it didn't seem possible, but there he was, there he is. What we actually say—this is the point I was making here—what we actually say is not necessarily what we believe, what we feel. I'll give an example of this, a story.

There is this journalist that I was always at war with. We got on personally quite well, but professionally, in public, we were always having to be pulled apart. And then there was the time I went to Rome to speak alongside Pope Francis in 2013. I went on the radio and talked about it afterwards. That night he rang me and said, I heard you on the radio. I thought he was gonna have a go at me, and he said, No, I was listening with my wife, who has cancer, and you know, some of the things you were saying really meant a lot to both of us. I just wanted to say that. I don't believe any of that stuff. By the way, he says, You know, I don't believe anybody who tells me that they know for sure that God exists, but neither do I believe those guys that say I'm sure he doesn't exist, either. I just don't have time for any of it. But still, I just wanted to say that to you. So I said, Thanks, and we had a bit of a conversation; and then about a month later, he rang me again and said, I'm doing a TV program about the state of the Church in Ireland, would you come on it? And I'm all buoyed up and encouraged by our newfound friendship and mutual understanding. I said, Yeah, sure. So I went on and he asked me a question about Catholicism and I started to go into kind of a Giussanian stream of consciousness or something. [*laughter*] He said, No, cut that stuff; I don't want hear any of that stuff. Just tell me about Church Catholicism, I want to talk to you about the Church. I said, I'm bored with that, I don't want to talk about that. So, the next thing we're having to be dug out of each other again, on-air. At the end of the show, I mean, it didn't get any better, and then at the end of the show I was sitting there, I'm taking off my mic, and I saw him up there, I didn't know what I was going to say to him, but I heard somebody else ask him about his wife, and I thought, I'd better ask him. When everybody had gone, I asked him, Is your wife okay? How is she doing? No, no, she's much better. Good. We kind of thawed out and he started to talk, and again, he kind of repeated a lot. He said, You're really good defending your corner. I said, Thanks, someday you might say that on-air. [*laughter*]

But we kind of had one of those conversations where you start here, and get to there in about three hours' time. Walking and stopping, walking and stopping; and he kept repeating, I don't believe in any of that stuff. He says, I don't believe anybody can tell me God exists, but I don't believe those who tell me he doesn't. I just don't have any time for that. But then he put his hand in his pocket and he said, But, you know, and he took out the rosary beads and said, I've had that in my pocket for the last six months, I don't know why. And that really got to me. How many other people are out there, who are on the TV all the time, saying certain things, but their heart is saying something else? And they have no way of being liberated? Because we're the ones who should be liberating them, but we're attacking them, or at least they think we are. We have to find a way of actually talking to them. I'm talking about me when I say "we." I mean, I have to find a way of not treating them like they're my enemy. That's really important. And a language that kind of affirms the heart, the longing of the heart, without trying to prove anything. Without trying to win the argument. But just talks the experience that we have openly and truthfully and trust it to be heard in the same spirit. Sometimes it won't. We can't expect it, we have no guarantee that it's going to be listened to in that way. But if we don't do it, we know it won't. That for me is a challenge now. I know I've been doing it wrong. I think of Albacete and think of that as his great gift, to be loved. There's nothing better. And so I wonder, before we finish, I want to read the poem from Patrick Kavanagh. Are we nearly finished? This is from "Canal Bank Walk."

Patrick Kavanagh, when he was fifty, had cancer and then wrote a series called "The Canal Poems," in which he realized that everything he'd thought before was kind of wrong. He realized the most important thing in life was what he called "not caring"; not caring what people think. Say what's in your heart, don't care what other people think. And this is really what I'm talking about, the words, and the limits of words, and the limits of arguments.

O unworn world enrapture me, encapture me in a web
Of fabulous grass and eternal voices by a beech,

Feed the gaping need of my senses, give me ad lib
To pray unselfconsciously with overflowing speech
For this soul needs to be honoured with a new dress woven
From green and blue things and arguments that cannot be proven.

Maniscalco: Thank you, John. [*applause*]

We've been given a treasure over this weekend. Talent, whatever you want to call it; a big gift. On Day One I told the volunteers—and by the way, we had about three hundred and fifty people who made this thing possible, who live the gratitude, gladness, and sacrifice. Sacrifice, which is a beautiful word even if often-times it scares us. If we only remembered the true meaning which is *sacrificium*, making things sacred, well then, maybe it would have a different impact on us. But this has been an experience of gratitude, gladness, and sacrifice. Memory now has to become the protagonist. I remember another conversation with Father Giussani, in which somebody thinking of the hard times to come, like tomorrow, which is another day and the Encounter is gone and we go back to our daily life. Somebody was saying, Yeah, the problem is holding up. And Giussani, who was a very intense human being, slammed his fist on the table and said, No! The problem is not holding up. The problem is the vividness of the origin. The problem is to keep the memory of the miracle that we experienced in the flesh. We can find the words, we use lots of words here, testimonies, poetry, even notes are like words. And yet, the most striking and visible thing was human faces, wasn't it? This is a promise. It calls for gratitude, gladness, and sacrifice, so that memory can keep building our life and the world around us. That's how I want to live. There are many ways to help us, from the tear-down tonight, to money which is now the most beautiful thing in the world, but it's part of reality. In fact, it was listed amongst the things here.

It is the reality of eating, drinking, waking, as you were saying—things which would appear to be banal; instead, they carry everything. The most striking thing for me, when I really met the companionship that generates this Encounter, was that everything was embraced. Everything was valuable, everything carried within it the Infinite, somehow. There were children, there were parents, grandparents, rich and poor, it's the whole world. It's the whole creation. Thank you, everybody.

www.ingramcontent.com/pod-product-compliance
Lightning Source LLC
Chambersburg PA
CBHW051833090426
42736CB00011B/1778

* 9 7 8 1 9 4 1 4 5 7 0 5 4 *